Dr Anne Szarewski is trained in the fields of family planning, genito-urinary medicine and colposcopy. She is currently a Clinical Research Fellow in Gynae-cological Oncology at the Imperial Cancer Research Fund, carrying out research related to cervical screening and the prevention of cancer. She is also a Senior Clinical Medical Officer in family planning at the Margaret Pyke Centre and a family planning doctor at the Marie Stopes Clinic.

The
Cervical
Smear Test

Dr Anne Szarewski

Illustrated by
Maggie Raynor

VERMILION
LONDON

First published in the United Kingdom by Optima in 1994

1 3 5 7 9 10 8 6 4 2

Copyright © Anne Szarewski 1994

This edition published in the United Kingdom in 1996 by Vermilion an imprint of Ebury Press

Random House UK Ltd
Random House
20 Vauxhall Bridge Road
London SW1V 2SA

Random House Australia (Pty) Ltd
20 Alfred Street, Milsons Point, Sydney,
New South Wales 2061, Australia

Random House New Zealand Limited
18 Poland Road, Glenfield,
Auckland 10, New Zealand

Random House, South Africa (Pty) Limited
Box 2263, Rosebank 2121, South Africa

Random House UK Limited Reg. No. 954009

A CIP catalogue record for this book is available from the British Library.

ISBN 0 09 181381 6

Printed and bound in Great Britain by Mackays of Chatham, plc

Papers used by Vermilion are natural, recyclable products made from wood grown in sustainable forests.

Contents

Introduction

Every year in this country hundreds of thousands of women have an abnormal smear. Around four thousand are told the sad news that they have cervical cancer, and roughly half of those women will die of the disease. Most of those deaths could be prevented by adequate screening and treatment. However, many women still do not go for cervical smears because they are frightened or do not understand the importance of the test. Those who do have a smear and are then told it is abnormal often think the worst, again through lack of knowledge and understanding.

The majority of women I have seen, both for smears and for colposcopy, have only a vague idea of what the tests are for, what they mean and what can be done if something is wrong. They want information but have often found it difficult to obtain. Then again, they may have read or been told certain things which are no longer thought to be true. This area of medicine has been changing rapidly and opinions which may have been thought correct a few years ago are not necessarily so now. Indeed, it is almost inevitable that some of the information presented in this book will be out of date within a short time of its publication.

It is frustrating that there are still many unanswered

1

or only partially answered questions in this field. We all find it difficult to deal with uncertainty. In this book I have not tried to give simple answers; where there are areas of doubt, I have stated them and presented the arguments for each point of view. I have tried to do this fairly, but inevitably my own biases will have crept in occasionally. I should make the point that the views I express in this book are mine and may not necessarily represent those of the Imperial Cancer Research Fund. In many cases this is because I am writing to you as an individual, and what is best for an individual may not always be applicable to, or indeed appropriate for, society as a whole.

Clinics are busy places and women often feel they cannot ask questions, or that the doctor will not have time to talk to them. Frequently, when faced with a doctor, women forget everything they wanted to ask anyway. I hope that a book such as this will provide information in a non-threatening way and then give you the confidence to ask questions which are specifically related to you, and which cannot be answered properly by any book or leaflet. Although I am sure the majority of readers will be women, it should not be forgotten that men are also involved, and may be worried for their partners: I hope this book will be of use to some of them, too.

I would like to thank Mr Pat Soutter who very kindly read through the whole book and made a number of constructive comments. Dr Peter Sasieni provided criticisms in an attempt to ensure that the book is 'epidemiologically and statistically correct' – or at least, acceptable. Any errors that remain are entirely mine. I would still be completely ignorant of research methods and statistics if it were not for the patience (sometimes very strained), help and example of Dr Jack

Cuzick and everyone in his department.

Acknowledgements are also due to: my editors, Hilary Foakes and Martin Bryant, Maggie Raynor for the line illustrations, the Photography and Illustration Centre at University College London and to Nicola Bion for her helpful and constructive comments.

1

What is the cervix? What is a smear?

The cervix is part of the womb, or uterus. The illustration opposite shows where the womb sits in the pelvis. You will see that it is connected to the ovaries by a pair of tubes, called the Fallopian tubes (after an Italian doctor called Fallopio). Eggs produced in the ovaries travel down these tubes to reach the womb. If you think of the womb as being like an upside-down pear, the cervix is the lower, narrower part. The womb is really just a box designed to contain a baby. The upper part, called the 'body' of the uterus, is where the baby is held and nourished when a woman is pregnant: it expands greatly during pregnancy as the baby gets bigger. The cervix, on the other hand, does not expand much until labour starts. Then it has to open up quickly, to let the baby out.

Both the body of the uterus and the cervix are made of muscle: the body of the uterus needs strong muscle tissue to push a baby out. Unfortunately, these strong muscles are also responsible for period cramps, which can be very painful in some women. The cervix also

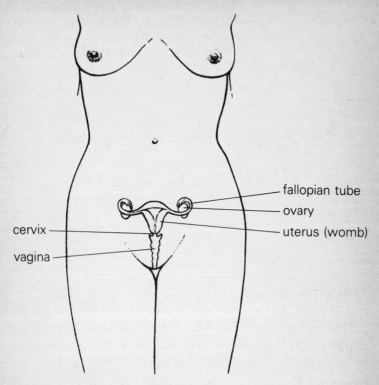

cervix

vagina

fallopian tube

ovary

uterus (womb)

Female reproductive organs

needs strong muscle, but for the opposite reason – to keep the growing, heavy baby in the womb until it is ready to come out. The cervix has two main muscle areas, called the internal os and the external os (see the illustration on page 6).

The muscle around the internal os is the innermost and strongest: it is the one primarily responsible for making sure the baby stays where it should. The external os, as its name suggests, is on the outside. Seen face on, the external os is a hole: in a woman who has not had children, or who has had them by Caesarean section, the hole is small, round and tight (see the

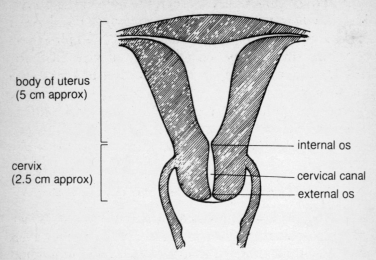

body of uterus
(5 cm approx)

cervix
(2.5 cm approx)

internal os

cervical canal

external os

Uterus and cervix

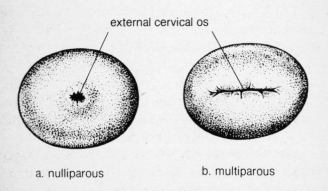

external cervical os

a. nulliparous

b. multiparous

View of the cervix, face on

illustration above). However, during childbirth, when the baby has to pass through it, the hole is stretched a great deal and does not return to its original shape and size. Instead, it becomes slit-shaped and wider than before.

Not only babies pass through the hole in the cervix: this is where the blood comes out when you have a period. Sperm use it to gain entry to the womb. If you have an intrauterine contraceptive device (IUD or IUCD) or coil fitted, it has to be pushed past the muscles of both the external os and the internal os, neither of which take too kindly to the idea – this is what can make the procedure uncomfortable. Unpleasant things such as infections can also creep in this way.

THE CERVIX UNDER A MAGNIFYING GLASS

Actually, we need more than a magnifying glass, we need to look through a microscope. This gives even more magnification, so that we can see the individual building blocks from which the cervix is made.

All the tissues in the body are made up of different types of cell. Cells are a little like fabrics: some are very delicate and fine, some are stronger and coarser. Just as we use delicate fabrics for clothes and strong ones for upholstery, so cells have different functions, too.

The body of the uterus is lined with soft, columnar (tall and narrow, like columns) cells (see the illustration on page 8). They are responsible for providing a growing pregnancy with nourishment: this has to arrive via blood vessels, so these cells have a good blood supply. The lining builds up each month in preparation for a possible pregnancy, but if none occurs, it comes off, bleeding while it does so. This is what you know as a period.

Meanwhile, the cells on the outside surface of both the cervix and the vagina have a much harder life. They are the 'front line', protecting the body of the womb from the outside world. They may be bombarded with infections and they must also withstand being hit

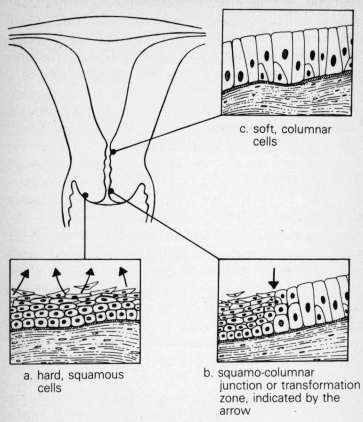

c. soft, columnar cells

a. hard, squamous cells

b. squamo-columnar junction or transformation zone, indicated by the arrow

Cells of the cervix and uterus

repeatedly during sex, so they are hard, squamous (meaning flat) cells. They don't have such a good blood supply – otherwise they would bleed every time you made love.

Of course, there has to be a point at which the two types of cell (squamous and columnar) meet, since the body of the uterus (womb) and the cervix are not actually physically separated from one another. Indeed, this area is called the squamo-columnar junction. In this area, soft columnar cells gradually change to become harder, squamous cells. Cells which are preoccupied with internal changes are more vulnerable to outside attack, so we will be looking at this area again in Chapter 2, when we discuss how abnormal cells appear.

The outside layers of cells are separated from the deeper, 'connective' tissues which contain blood vessels and glands by a continuous layer of cells called the basement membrane (see the illustration below). This acts as a physical barrier and will be very important when we discuss the development of invasive cancer in Chapter 6.

When seen under a microscope, the surface of the cervix is not smooth, but has many tiny folds, rather like the irregular pattern of a coastline. The 'bays' are

Squamous layer of cells separated from the connective tissue by the basement membrane

called crypts and, if they become blocked off, they form little fluid-filled cysts, rather like a lagoon which becomes a lake. They can be seen and sometimes felt as little bumps on the surface of the cervix and are called Nabothian follicles, after the doctor who first described them.

WHAT IS A CERVICAL SMEAR?

A cervical smear is a simple screening test for early changes in the cells which may lead to cervical cancer. Cervical cancer is theoretically totally preventable by screening, because these early changes can be picked up long before a proper cancer will ever develop. Despite this, 2000 women die of cervical cancer in the UK every year, many of them because they have not taken the opportunity to have a smear.

It is important to realise that the test is not looking primarily for proper cancer cells. If that was all it could pick up, it would be a waste of everyone's time – including yours – because many women would still die. The whole point of the test is that the early changes are not actually cancer and are completely curable. Indeed, a screening test, by definition, needs to be done when you are completely well, *before* you have noticed any symptoms.

Any woman who has *ever* had sex should have regular smears. Although cervical cancer can very rarely occur in virgins, it is usually found in women who are or have been sexually active. I shall be discussing the possible causes of cervical cancer in Chapters 7 and 8, so will not dwell on them further here.

WHAT IS THE EXAMINATION LIKE?

'I was terrified when I went in, but I knew I should try and relax. I kept saying to myself, relax, relax, but it was impossible. I was afraid of what was going to happen.'

A cervical smear involves a vaginal examination. Unfortunately, there is just no other way. You will be asked to lie down on a couch, having removed your panties. Your feet will be pointing towards a light, which will be used to illuminate your vagina (front passage). The doctor or nurse will need to use an instrument called a speculum to gently push apart the sides of your vagina, in order to be able to see your cervix. The speculum can be made of metal or plastic (see the illustration on page 12), and its two halves will be closed together while it is being inserted, and then opened up once the instrument is inside.

If the speculum is made of metal, its natural state will be freezing cold. Doctors and nurses can forget this, so remind them! The instrument can easily be warmed by putting it under the hot tap or keeping it on a warm radiator. Once the instrument is warm, you will find it easier to relax and the whole process will become simpler.

Did I mention the word 'relax'? Well, difficult though it is, you should try. The more tense you are, the more difficult it will be to open the speculum inside you (after all, you will be positively pushing against it) and the more uncomfortable it will feel. How can you relax? Well, for a start, try not to arrange to have your smear on a day when you have an important meeting at work, or are going to be under stress for other reasons. Bring a friend with you, perhaps, at least to sit with in the waiting room.

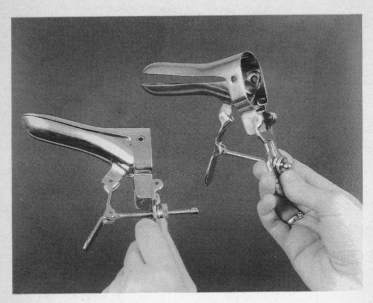

A speculum, closed and open

It is very important that the person taking the smear can get a good view of your cervix: a sample from the wrong place will be of no use and will only result in you having to go through the procedure once again.

Once the cervix is in view, a spatula is gently wiped across it to collect some loose cells. A bewildering variety of instruments can be used to take smears, ranging from wooden spatulas to nylon brushes. We will discuss these in more detail in Chapter 3.

Once the smear has been taken, the speculum is removed and, from your point of view, the procedure is over. You will find, perhaps to your surprise, that the entire event has taken less than five minutes.

'I expected it to be so much worse. My sister said it was really painful.'

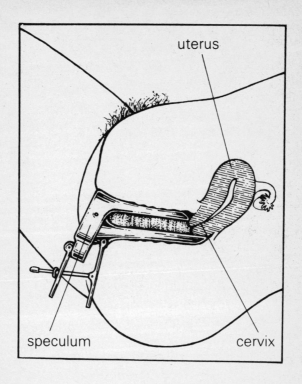

uterus

speculum   cervix

Speculum in place during a vaginal examination

'*I was so embarrassed that he was a man. I hadn't thought about that before at all. It was different when I just had the measles.*'

Many women are frightened of having a smear because they don't know what it will involve, or, even worse, a friend has had a bad experience and has kindly passed all the details on. I have heard awful stories of rough examinations and unsympathetic doctors or nurses. But they are still in a minority. The chances are that you will be in the care of someone who does know what they are doing.

From top to bottom: Cytobrush; Jordan/Rolon spatula; Aylesbury spatula; Ayre spatula

'*I was in such a state, I was shaking. I was still determined to try and have it done. But when I went in to the nurse, she just talked to me for a few minutes, explaining what the examination involved. Then she gave me a leaflet to read. She said I should come back another day, when I'd read the information. She suggested I bring a friend with me as well. I did go back the following week and brought my sister with me. She made me have a gin and tonic before we went into the clinic! I felt much better and it was OK.*'

If you are extremely worried, mention this to the doctor or nurse at the start of the appointment. In some cases, they may suggest that you return another day, bringing a friend, or even that they give you a mild tranquilliser. One bad experience can make future examinations ten times more difficult, so it is worth making sure you are as prepared as possible. Incidentally, if you have had a traumatic event in the past, such as a rough examination, or if you have been raped and examinations are very emotionally charged for you, mention it in advance.

If you are uncomfortable with a male doctor, ask for a woman. If there seems to be no choice at your doctor's practice, go to a different one, or to a clinic. You are perfectly entitled to do this, even if you stay with your normal GP for the rest of your care. If you really feel you can't go through with an examination, say so. You can always come back another time. Although smears are for your protection, you shouldn't feel you have been forced to have one. They may be advisable, but they are not compulsory.

WHAT HAPPENS TO THE SMEAR?

The cells are transferred on to a glass slide by wiping the spatula across it. The cells cannot survive for long like this, so they have to be 'fixed' or preserved using an alcohol solution. You may see this being poured on to the slide, or you may see a spray being used instead. Once this has been done, the smear can be kept safely for a long time. It is sent to a laboratory where the cells are stained with various dyes to show up their features more clearly.

The cells are then examined under a microscope by specially trained technicians and doctors called cytologists. The word 'cytology' simply means the study of cells (*cyto* means cell in Greek, while *ology* means the study of). The technicians look at each slide. Any they think may show an abnormality is then double-checked by a doctor. Although it may take weeks for you to hear the result, during most of that time your slide is sitting idle in a pile, waiting for its turn. The actual process of checking it takes about twenty minutes on average.

A report is then sent back to your doctor or clinic. Usually the report comes back on the original smear form, though some laboratories now produce computer printouts. Whichever method is used, the reporting is mostly standardised. Although most women never get to see their smear report, there is no reason why this should be so. One of my aims in this book is to explain the report form and the reporting system so that you will be able to understand your own smear result.

THE CERVICAL SMEAR FORM

The illustration on page 17 shows the current, nationally used smear form. The left-hand side is for your personal details, your name, address, date of birth, registration number. Also given are the name and address of your doctor. If it is not your GP who is taking the smear, his/her details are given anyway so that they also can be sent a copy of the result.

On the right-hand side there are details about your relevant medical history. The date of the current smear is given and also the date of your last smear. This allows the laboratory to check the time interval between your smears: some labs may now reject smears taken at more frequent intervals than they consider appropriate – we shall discuss this again in Chapter 9. More helpfully, if there is a query about your current result, they may be able to recheck the slide sent to them previously (only if both were sent to the same laboratory, of course).

The date of your last period is important because the appearance of the cells varies at different times in the menstrual cycle. Cells also look different if you have gone past the change of life (the menopause), so if the

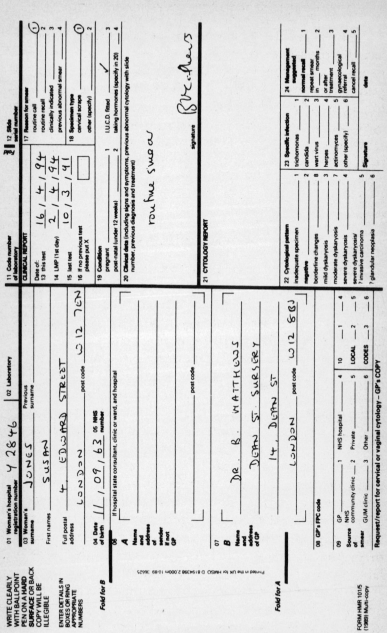

Smear form, with some details completed

11 Code number of laboratory				Fold
CLINICAL REPORT				
Date of: 13 this test	16	4	94	
14 LMP (1st day)	2	4	94	
15 last test	10	3	91	
16 If no previous test please put X				

Close-up of section dealing with date of test and last menstrual period (LMP)

date of the last period is several months or years ago, the cytologist will be alerted to this.

Section 19 gives other medical details, for example whether you are pregnant, have recently had a baby (postnatal), or have an IUD (intrauterine contraceptive device, or coil). An IUD can sometimes make the cells look slightly unusual and so the cytologist needs to be aware if you have one. Hormones, whether they are being taken for contraceptive, hormone replacement or other reasons, may alter the expected appearance of the cells (particularly since they may not look 'right' for the supposed time of a natural menstrual cycle). More details will then be written in section 20 (see opposite).

19 Condition				
pregnant	1	I.U.C.D. fitted	✓	3
post-natal (under 12 weeks)	2	taking hormones (specify in 20)		4

Section 19

12	**Slide** **serial number**		

17	**Reason for smear**		
	routine call	_____	①
	routine recall	_____	2
	clinically indicated	_____	3
	previous abnormal smear	_____	4

18	**Specimen type**		
	cervical scrape	_____	①
	other (specify)	_____	2

Sections 17 and 18 together

Section 17 tells the lab whether this is a routine smear, or whether there is a special reason for having one at this time, for example that you have had an abnormal smear in the past, or that the doctor feels you should have one because of abnormal bleeding. Once again, more details will be given in section 20.

Section 18 is important mainly if the smear is being taken from the vagina for some reason instead of from the cervix, for example following a hysterectomy, in which case 'other' will be ticked.

Section 20 is a blank area for the doctor or nurse to write in anything they feel is relevant. For example, this is where they would explain which type of hormones

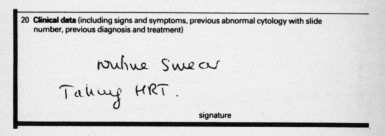

20 **Clinical data** (including signs and symptoms, previous abnormal cytology with slide
number, previous diagnosis and treatment)

routine smear

Taking HRT.

signature

Section 20 with some details filled in

you were taking, or that you had been treated for an abnormal smear in the past.

The bottom left-hand section (22) gives the smear result. For example, if it is negative, the number 2, opposite 'negative', will be circled. If the sample was inadequate and needs to be repeated, the number 1, opposite 'inadequate specimen', will be circled. I shall discuss the rest of the classifications in section 22 in the next chapter.

Section 23 is used if any infections were noticed on the smear. For example, if candida (thrush) is picked up on the smear, the number 2 will be circled. Infections are discussed in more detail in Chapter 3.

Section 21 is another blank space where the cytologist can write any extra comments about your smear. Often there will be nothing written in it; however, this section can cause a lot of anxiety and misunderstand-

---

21 CYTOLOGY REPORT

Endocervical cells seen

22 Cytological pattern		23 Specific infection		24 Management suggested	
inadequate specimen	1	trichomonas	1	normal recall	(1)
negative	(2)	candida	(2)	repeat smear in ___ months	2
borderline changes	8	wart virus	3	or after treatment	3
mild dyskaryosis	3	herpes	4		
moderate dyskaryosis	7	actinomyces	5	gynaecological referral	4
severe dyskaryosis	4	other (specify)	6	cancel recall	5
severe dyskaryosis/ ? invasive carcinoma	5	**Signature**		**date**	
? glandular neoplasia	6				

Sections 21, 22, 23 and 24

ing. The most common phrases you are likely to see are 'no endocervical cells seen', 'endocervical cells seen' and 'inflammatory changes'. These terms are explained in Chapter 3. It is not unknown for the comments to be so technical that other doctors cannot understand them either ... I hope that this book will make at least the more common ones less threatening.

In section 24 the cytologist recommends what course of action should be taken following this smear. For example, if it is negative, they will tick 'normal recall'. The timing of your next smear will depend on what 'normal recall' is in your area: it varies according to government guidelines, local resources and doctors' opinions (not necessarily in that order). This will be discussed fully in Chapter 9. If you need further investigations, number 4, 'gynaecological referral', will be ticked or circled. Sometimes an infection has obscured the smear and a repeat will be required after the infection has been treated: in this case number 3 will be circled.

Your doctor may choose not to follow the recommendation given on the smear form: it is, after all, only 'management suggested'. If there is a discrepancy, or if you are unsure of what is happening, ask for an explanation, don't just go home and worry about it.

Obviously, the most important part of the form is section 22, which tells you whether your smear is negative or not. Let us now look at the meaning of the phrase 'positive smear'.

2

What is a
positive smear?

*'I opened the envelope and there it was: my smear
was positive. I was going to die. Why me? What had
I done? I burst into tears.'*

*'There was a long letter and an information sheet,
explaining all about cell changes. The words swam
in front of my eyes, I felt dizzy. All I could think
about were those two words, "positive smear".'*

The term 'positive smear' must be one of the most
emotive in medicine. And yet, all it refers to is a smear
that is not normal or negative. The term 'positive'
encompasses every grade of abnormality, from borderline abnormal cells right through to cancer. Why do so
many women immediately assume the worst? In the UK
there are probably about 300,000 'positive' smear
results every year. And yet the number of women who
are found to have cancer is about 4000 – of whom
many have not had a smear at all. So a 'positive' smear
result is *very* unlikely to mean you have cancer. But
what *does* it mean?

ABNORMAL CELL CHANGES

In Chapter 1 I looked at the different types of cells, or building blocks, which make up the cervix. You may remember that there are two types, the soft columnar ones and the hard, squamous ones. Where soft columnar cells are exposed to the outside world, they gradually adapt by changing into tougher

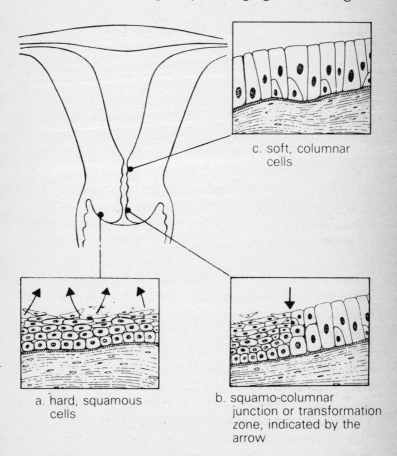

c. soft, columnar cells

a. hard, squamous cells

b. squamo-columnar junction or transformation zone, indicated by the arrow

Cells of the cervix and uterus

squamous cells. This happens around the area of the cervical canal and is called the squamo-columnar junction. The process, which is quite normal, is called squamous metaplasia (metaplasia means change, or transformation). The area in which this change, or transformation, takes place is also called the transformation zone (see the illustration on page 23).

Cells which are changing are occupied and 'off-guard'. Thus, these cells are the ones most vulnerable to attack; they may start to change in the 'wrong' way and, if so, eventually could become cancer cells.

These changes do not occur overnight; in fact, it is a very slow process. It has been estimated that it probably takes around ten years for normal cells to become cancer cells.

Cells which are starting to change abnormally can be distinguished from normal ones under the microscope. They tend to be smaller and have a larger nucleus relative to the rest of the cell. The nucleus is like a brain, telling the cell what to do. The illustration below gives you an idea of the different appearances of normal and abnormal cells.

There are a couple of different terms used to describe cells which are changing abnormally. The oldest term, dysplasia, comes from the Greek *dys* which means bad or abnormal, and *plasia* which means change. Dysplasia therefore means abnormal change. Thus

Normal cells   Mild dyskaryosis   Moderate dyskaryosis   Severe dyskaryosis   Cancer cells

```
22 Cytological pattern
inadequate specimen      _____  1
negative                 _____  2
borderline changes       _____  8
mild dyskaryosis         _____  (3)
moderate dyskaryosis     _____  7
severe dyskaryosis       _____  4
severe dyskaryosis/
? invasive carcinoma     _____  5
? glandular neoplasia    _____  6
```

Section 22 of smear form

'mild dysplasia' means mild abnormal change, 'moderate dysplasia' means moderately abnormal change, 'severe dysplasia' means severely abnormal change. They represent increasingly abnormal stages of change in the cells, but none of them is cancer.

Another term, adopted more recently in the UK, is dyskaryosis (see the illustration above). Once again, *dys* means bad or abnormal, while the word *karyon* means nucleus. This term, therefore, emphasises the changes that occur in the nucleus of the cell. Nevertheless, it is synonymous with dysplasia, so 'mild dyskaryosis' is equivalent to mild dysplasia, 'moderate dyskaryosis' to moderate dysplasia and 'severe dyskaryosis' to severe dysplasia. Most other countries still use the term dysplasia, so you may easily come across both.

If you see an old smear form, you may notice the term 'carcinoma-in-situ' (see the illustration on page 26). This sounds awful: the Latin *in situ* means 'which has not spread', so the term means 'cancer which has not spread'. However, it was used only to mean severe dysplasia or severe dyskaryosis where the cytologist felt

23 EVIDENCE OF NEOPLASIA CYTOLOGICAL PATTERN SUGGESTS:		24 INFLAMMATION		25 FURTHER INVESTIGATION SUGGESTED	
Inadequate specimen	1	Severe Inflammatory Change	1	Repeat smear in months	1
Negative	2	Trichomonas	2	or after treatment	2
Mild dysplasia	3	Candida	4	Colposcopy	16
Severe dysplasia/ carcinoma-in-situ	(4)	Viral	8	Cervical biopsy	4
Carcinoma-in-situ/? invasive	5	Signature		Uterine curettage	8
? Glandular neoplasia	6	Fold		date	

Old smear form showing 'carcinoma-in-situ'

it *might* soon become cancer. It has been withdrawn
because it caused a great deal of anxiety and confusion.
However, to allow a cytologist to differentiate between
'severe dyskaryosis – not too much to worry about',
and 'severe dyskaryosis – hurry up and investigate', a
new category has been introduced: 'severe dyskaryosis/
?invasive cancer' (see the illustration on page 25).

Please don't allow these complicated arguments to
obscure the main point. Cells which are changing
abnormally are *absolutely not* cancer until they move
on a stage from severe dyskaryosis. And indeed, many
of them will never become cancer. The whole beauty of
the smear test is that the cells can be identified when
they are still completely harmless: they have the potential to become cancer, but they won't do so for a long
time, if at all. Thus they, and any chance of cancer, can
be removed easily and well in time.

ANOTHER CLASSIFICATION SYSTEM – CIN

I'm afraid so. Just as you thought you'd got it sorted out
in your mind, here is another term. However, this one is
not so different from the others, only it doesn't refer to
individual cells, it refers to their arrangement in the cervix.

CIN stands for Cervical Intra-epithelial Neoplasia. If you remember that *plasia* means change, then *neo* means new, and so neoplasia means new change. *Intra* means in, and epithelial refers to the outer layers of cells which act as a protective covering for the blood vessels and glands (known as connective tissues, see page 9). Cervical simply means 'of the cervix'. So CIN means 'new changes occurring in the outer layers of cells of the cervix'.

This classification refers to the way abnormal cells are arranged in the cervix. If only one third of the thickness of the epithelium (outer layers of skin) is involved, this is the first stage of abnormality, CIN 1. If two thirds are involved, that is CIN 2. If the whole thickness consists of abnormal cells, that is CIN 3. As you may have realised, this cannot be seen on a smear, because a smear consists only of loose cells. So, to see CIN under the microscope, you need a small piece of the cervix, called a biopsy. This will be

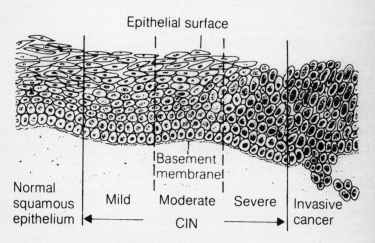

Changes in the cells of the cervix, from normality through CIN to an invasive cancer

discussed in more detail in Chapter 4.

In fact, CIN 1 can be thought of as equivalent to mild dysplasia/dyskaryosis, CIN 2 as equivalent to moderate dysplasia/dyskaryosis, and CIN 3 as equivalent to severe dysplasia/dyskaryosis.

Because CIN is short and quick to say, it is often used instead of dyskaryosis or dysplasia. For example, a smear showing 'mild dyskaryosis' may be referred to as a 'CIN 1 smear'. Strictly speaking this is incorrect because, as mentioned above, it is not possible to diagnose CIN from loose cells on a smear. Don't worry about it at present, but I shall return to this concept again later.

> 'I was sitting in the surgery and the doctor was trying to explain what was wrong with my smear. I know she said "cancer", I heard it. I can't understand why she was trying to make it sound less serious. I've got cancer and that's that.'

Once again, it is important to stress that, by definition, no grade of CIN is cancer. It has sometimes been called 'pre-cancer' to emphasise that it is 'before cancer', but the term is self-defeating because the very presence of the word 'cancer' causes panic. I know this is beginning to get repetitive, but these are just cells which have the *potential* to develop into cancer over a long period of time.

I HAVE AN ABNORMAL SMEAR, WHAT HAPPENS NEXT?

> 'I sat and looked at the letter for five days. It just said, "There is no cause for alarm. Please come and discuss your smear result with the doctor at your earliest convenience." But when I rang the surgery,

they said I couldn't be seen for five days. I couldn't work, I couldn't sleep, I didn't want to see anyone. I didn't want to tell my family or my friends. I didn't know what to say.'

'The doctor was very helpful, explained that it wasn't anything serious but I would need to have a special examination. He gave me some leaflets to read and said I could always come back if I had any questions. The information helped a lot, as I was able to read it when I was feeling a little better. I did go back to him and I borrowed a book from the library. I wanted to understand exactly what was going on.'

The most common reaction to being informed of an abnormal smear seems to be that of blind panic. Why? Because doctors, health educators, schools, the media, have all failed to get across the simple message that an abnormal smear does not mean cancer, that it is just an early warning of something which may – or may not – develop later. Many standard letters also do not give the exact result, they just say the smear is abnormal and you should come in to discuss it. This would be fine if you were able to discuss it straight away, but the chances are you will have to wait a few days, imagining the worst all the time. To my mind it is less frightening to know straight away in the letter exactly what is going on – provided some information is included to explain the result. However, the chances are that you will need to see your doctor to find out.

'When I got the letter, I was really worried. Only last month my friend Angela was talking about someone who went through all this last year and had a terrible

time. There was a mix-up over the results, she wasn't seen when she should have been and in the end she nearly got cancer. She's fine now, but apparently she's very bitter. Angela said she often talks about it.'

'The next day I went in to work. I hadn't intended to mention it at all, but it just came out, I couldn't stop myself. My boss, Julia, was so sympathetic, she said she'd had an abnormal smear three years ago. She told me all about the hospital and the examination I would have to have. It made me feel much better, as she seemed to be quite OK about it. She said it hadn't been nearly as bad as she had expected beforehand and told me not to worry too much.'

While you are waiting for your appointment with the doctor, use the delay to prepare yourself. Get as much information as you can, from leaflets, books, organisations. Talk to your friends. You will almost certainly be surprised to find how many women you know who have been through the experience. Around 300,000 women every year in this country have some kind of abnormal smear, so you are certainly not alone. Bear in mind, though, when you talk to friends, that those few who have had bad experiences usually have the most vivid memories. If you hear horror stories, try to find someone who had a better experience, to redress the balance a little.

When you see the doctor, make sure you are told exactly what your smear result was. There is no reason at all why you should not see your own result form. Your doctor may be worried that it will frighten you because you won't understand it. One of the purposes of this book is to help you understand smear reports, so that you know why you are having investigations. Many women find it more frightening not to be shown the report: after all, why is there something to hide?

Once you have established what grade of abnormality the smear showed, you will need to discuss what is going to happen next. This is very straightforward if the result showed moderate or severe dyskaryosis (or, of course, in the rare event that the result suggests cancer): you will be referred to a hospital for colposcopy.

Colposcopy is simply a way of taking a closer look at the cervix through a large magnifying glass, and is described in detail in Chapter 4. Three important things happen at colposcopy. The first is that the doctor can, with a good degree of accuracy, tell whether or not you have cancer. The chances are that you won't have cancer and so you can be reassured of this immediately. If everything looks completely normal, you will also be told that straight away. If there is an abnormal-looking area present, the grade of abnormality can be suggested, but is not guaranteed to be accurate. For this reason, a tiny piece, or biopsy, will be taken, to be checked in a laboratory. If you recall our discussion of CIN, this little piece of the cervix is what allows the grade of CIN to be determined.

If colposcopy and biopsy confirm the presence of CIN 2 or 3 (the second or third stage of abnormal cells), it is likely you will be advised to have treatment, and I shall be looking at the various options in Chapter 5.

The dilemma of the mildly abnormal smear

Things are not so straightforward if the result is borderline or mild dyskaryosis. This means the cells are

showing only borderline or mild abnormalities. Should
you have a colposcopy, or should you simply have
another smear in six months? The medical world is
currently at war over this issue. Some people argue
that, since mild abnormalities often go away on their
own, why investigate straight away, why not give it
time? And even if a mild abnormality is there, nothing
is going to happen in six months, or even a year. After
all, the cell changes occur very slowly, over several
years, not six or even twelve months. And some women
are made more anxious by having to go to the hospital
for further investigations, while they would be less
worried by only having to have a repeat smear. All this
is true.

The other argument is this: mild abnormalities are
certainly not dangerous, and can easily be left alone,
but can we be sure that the abnormality really is mild?
A number of studies have shown that up to a third of
smears showing 'mild dyskaryosis' are wrong. When
these women have a colposcopy, they are found to have
CIN 2 or even CIN 3, despite the smear suggesting only
a mild abnormality. The same applies to about a fifth
of smears which show borderline changes. Can we be
sure it is safe to wait? And some women are made more
anxious by not knowing exactly what is going on; they
would prefer to be investigated. All this is also true.

So what should you, the person in the middle, do?
Well, partly it does depend on how you see it. What will
make you feel better, having repeat smears, or being
investigated? The odds are certainly in favour of the
fact that nothing adverse will happen to you, whichever course you choose.

But what about those smears which are wrong,
where you already have CIN 2 or 3? This is the main
problem, as I see it, and this is the reason I tend towards

recommending investigation. Even though the odds are in your favour, I dislike uncertainty. Once you *know* you have only CIN 1, fine, don't have it treated; wait and see if it gets better on its own. But you don't know that from the smear, you can only know that after a colposcopy and biopsy, when they have looked under the microscope at the arrangement of the cells.

I have suggested that proven CIN 1 does not need treatment: why? Remember that CIN 1 has got to go through CIN 2 and CIN 3 before cancer can develop. It isn't going to do that very fast, it will take years. Sometimes the cells will change back and become normal on their own. Indeed, it has been shown that just taking the tiny biopsy often helps a small area of abnormality to improve, perhaps because it stimulates the body's immune response to fight back. And if it doesn't get better and you go on to develop CIN 2? The treatment is very simple and you are still not in any danger.

Some women prefer to avoid medical intervention, and to try homeopathy or another type of alternative medicine instead. This is fine for CIN 1. There is no scientific evidence either way, but, as I have said, watching and waiting at this stage will not do any harm. And it may make you feel you are doing something positive to help yourself.

Incidentally, you may be wondering why CIN 2 or even 3 need treatment, when neither is cancer. The reason is that they seem less likely to go away on their own and may get worse. It could certainly be argued that a small area of CIN 2 could be left a while. But since we do not know the precise time-scale of cell changes, if CIN 3 is there already, it might just tip over into early cancer if left too long.

Does CIN 1 ever need treatment? Yes, sometimes.

The most important reason is if you feel too anxious about leaving it, even after reading this book. But make sure you have considered what the treatment involves, simple though it is; read Chapter 5. The second reason is if the area involved is large, because it is less likely to get better on its own. Also, if it becomes even larger, it may become technically difficult to treat, should the cells move on to CIN 2 or 3. In such a case, although there is no hard and fast rule, I often feel it would be better to treat sooner rather than later. Another reason to favour treatment is if you will not be able to return for monitoring. Say you have a job which takes you around the world for long periods of time, or you are going to emigrate somewhere where the medical facilities may be poor – then you may just prefer to be treated and get the whole thing over and done with.

Of course, what I have described is an ideal. You may not be offered a choice between repeat smears or immediate colposcopy at all. Financial constraints have meant that in most areas nowadays you will not be offered a colposcopy after one borderline or mildly abnormal smear. Indeed, you may not be offered investigation after two, but have to wait until after three – that could be a year later if they are six months apart. Interestingly, there is now conflicting evidence about the cost of each approach: for a number of years it has been argued that it is cheaper to repeat smears before referral, but recently it has been suggested that by the time a woman has had several repeat smears, possibly ending up with colposcopy anyway, it would be cheaper to offer colposcopy straight away.

So, again, what should you do? Actually, I do not think it is too unreasonable to have a borderline smear repeated six months later. If it is normal, you should have another one in six months and, if that is also negative, at yearly intervals thereafter. If it is abnormal, I would then recommend colposcopy. However, if the smear shows mild dyskaryosis, I would be happier to do a colposcopy after the first abnormal smear.

What if the choice is not available in your area? Well, you can ask your GP to refer you somewhere else. Policies are very variable and you may find that a clinic in another district will see you, even if you have to wait a couple of months. Since a repeat smear takes six months, you are still better off even if it takes that long to have the colposcopy. And nothing is likely to happen to you in such a short time; keep reminding yourself that cell changes occur very slowly.

The obvious solution to all these problems would be a way of differentiating (without resorting to colposcopy) between those women who really do have only a mild abnormality and could wait, and those who need to be investigated now. In fact, there are two possibilities on the horizon, one already available. Cervicography is a way of taking a photograph of the cervix, showing up any abnormal areas. It can be done in any GP surgery or clinic and the examination is not too different from a smear. The photographs are looked at by an expert who can decide which women need to be seen soonest. The other possibility is a new form of testing based on the presence of certain kinds of wart virus. Both of these are discussed further in Chapter 11.

'I had had two smears which showed abnormal cells. When I went to the doctor, I was already psyched up to the idea of a hospital appointment. I'd read about colposcopy and I was prepared for it. I was completely thrown when he said I was going to have to have another smear, again in six months' time.

Apparently, the waiting list couldn't cope if everyone was seen sooner. I went home, but I was upset. Then I got angry. My health was more important than a stupid waiting list. My first thought was, I'll go private, and I even rang up a doctor recommended by a friend. It would cost me nearly £300. I don't have insurance and I'm not made of money. Peter said he'd find the money, that of course I should have the best. But I sat down and thought about it again. I decided to go back to the doctor. I was ready for a fight, but he immediately said, "I can see you're upset." I burst into tears, I couldn't help it. He said he'd do his best to get me an appointment: one of the consultants at another hospital was able to squeeze people in sometimes. It was quite a lot further away, would I mind? Actually, the hospital wasn't far from where Peter works, so it was better in a way. Two months later I went for my appointment. Peter took the afternoon off and came with me. It was a good thing he did: it turned out that I already had CIN 3, much more serious than my smear showed. The consultant booked me in for treatment and it was all got rid of in time. But it's not right I had to fight to be seen. What about women who are frightened of making a fuss?'

'The doctor explained that when a smear just showed borderline changes, it might sometimes be a mistake, or the changes would go back to normal on their own. When she told me that it depended on people looking down microscopes, trying to decide whether things looked completely normal or not, I could see it might be difficult. She suggested I have a repeat smear in six months first: if that still showed cell changes she would send me to the hospital. I was

happy with that, the hospital appointment seemed a bit frightening, especially if it might not be necessary. My next smear was OK, I was so relieved. The doctor said I'd better have another one in six months, just to be sure. That was normal as well. I have smears every year now and they've all been fine. I'm glad it was all so easy in the end.'

3

What does this mean? A look at some technical terms

NO ENDOCERVICAL CELLS SEEN. NEGATIVE

Alternatively, you may see, 'Endocervical cells seen. Negative.' Whichever way round it is put, the result seems to be anxiety.

'I thought, "What are these things they've seen? Why have I got them?"'

'Does that mean my smear is no good? What didn't they see? Will I have to have another one?'

Comments about the presence or absence of endo-cervical cells are the most frequent phrases you are likely to see handwritten in section 21 (see smear form, opposite).

Endocervical cells are similar to the soft, columnar cells that are normally found lining the inside of the womb. They are present at the squamo-columnar junction (see page 8), where some of them start to change into flat squamous cells. In Chapter 2, I

21 **CYTOLOGY REPORT**

No endocervical cells seen

22 **Cytological pattern**		23 **Specific infection**		24 **Management suggested**	
inadequate specimen	1	trichomonas	1		
negative	2	candida	2	normal recall	1
borderline changes	8	wart virus	3	repeat smear in ___ months	2
mild dyskaryosis	3	herpes	4	or after treatment	3
moderate dyskaryosis	7	actinomyces	5	gynaecological referral	4
severe dyskaryosis	4	other (specify)	6	cancel recall	5
severe dyskaryosis/ ? invasive carcinoma	5	**Signature**		**date**	
? glandular neoplasia	6				

Smear form result: negative

discussed the importance of this area, since it is the place where abnormal changes are likely to begin.

If this area is important, it would be nice to know that it has been checked by the smear. One of the ways in which we can tell it has been checked is to see endocervical cells. Other markers are columnar cells which are undergoing squamous metaplasia (that is, which have started the process of changing into flat, squamous cells). They look subtly different from endocervical cells, but are also present at the squamo-columnar junction. Cervical mucus can also be seen on a smear, and is another indicator that the squamo-columnar junction has been checked. In practice, if cytologists see any of these three markers, they will simply write 'endocervical cells seen' on the form.

You would not believe the arguments that have been going on for years about the importance (or otherwise) of seeing squamo-columnar junction markers (which I shall refer to collectively as endocervical cells from now on). The argument goes like this: if endocervical cells are so important, then we should be able to show that smears which have them are more likely also to be abnormal. Alternatively, we should be able to show that smears without endocervical cells are more likely to be falsely reassuring, that the woman may have an abnormal area on her cervix, but it has been missed. This second option is impractical, because every woman having a smear would also have to have a colposcopy at the same time (see Chapter 4).

So, we are left with studies which look at different ways of taking smears, comparing abnormality rates with the pick-up of endocervical cells.

The illustration on page 41 shows a selection of instruments which have all been designed to take smears. You may also want to look back at the photograph on page 14 of Chapter 1. The traditional Ayre spatula has gradually been replaced in the UK by the Aylesbury, which is more pointed. The idea of the point is to try to reach the squamo-columnar junction, even if it is not on the outside surface of the cervix, but further up inside the cervical canal. (This is more likely in slightly older women, over the age of 35.) The Jordan/Rolon spatula and the Cytobrush are further refinements on this idea. The Cytobrush should be used as well as, not instead of, a spatula, because on its own it doesn't sample the outside surface of the cervix at all. This is the ultimate belt and braces approach, covering every possible place where the squamo-columnar junction could be. And, indeed, many studies have shown that if you are interested in endocervical cells, the Cytobrush plus spatula combination picks up cells that other methods just cannot reach.

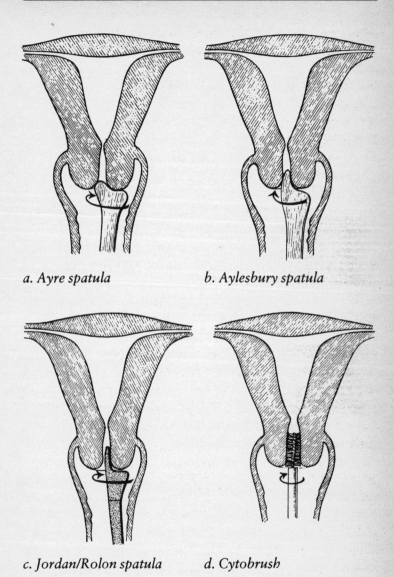

a. Ayre spatula   *b. Aylesbury spatula*

c. Jordan/Rolon spatula   *d. Cytobrush*

The difficulty is proving that it matters. Logically, from our previous discussion about the squamo-columnar junction, it should make a difference. You should find that you pick up more abnormalities with a Cytobrush–spatula combination. And some studies do indeed suggest that is the case. But others don't, and therein lies the problem. There are probably as many studies saying it makes no difference as those saying it does. In many countries, doctors have decided that, until there is conclusive proof it is *not* important, they will do their best to pick up endocervical cells. In this country, the opposite view has generally prevailed – that until conclusively proven that it *does* make a difference, it will not be considered important.

As a result many laboratories have not been reporting whether endocervical cells are present or not. However, in recent years, there has been a shift towards reporting their presence, though this is by no means universal and the argument is still raging. It must be said that part of the argument in this country is financial: if it is decided that endocervical cells are important, smears not containing them would have to be labelled as inadequate. Women would then have to be recalled for repeat smears: this could involve around 20 or even 30 per cent of the smears taken and therefore a lot of time and money.

As far as I can see, the issue of picking up more abnormalities is still unresolved. But there is another, very good reason for reporting endocervical cells: quality control.

Cells from the outside surface of the cervix are pretty much identical to those from the vagina: they are all flat, squamous cells. So, if a smear does not contain any of the markers of the squamo-columnar junction (referred to collectively as endocervical cells), it could have been taken from anywhere in the vagina, and it may not even have included the cervix at all. The laboratory will simply not be able to tell the difference.

In 1993, a nurse in a general practice surgery was found to be using a tongue depressor to take smears. She had apparently been doing this for nearly two years before it came to light, and over a thousand women were asked to have another smear. It is likely that many of the smears she had taken did not contain endocervical cells; if someone had thought to enquire why this was, she might have been discovered earlier.

Personally, I think this is the more important issue. Even if you train doctors and nurses to take smears, you cannot guarantee that they will all be good at it. Some may have been competent to start with, but may now be 'rusty' due to lack of practice. Others may just be careless. In practical terms, the only way to find out if smears are being taken incorrectly is to see whether a doctor or nurse has a particularly high 'no endocervical cells seen' rate. If they do, the laboratory can ask how they are taking their smears and suggest ways in which they can improve their technique.

What if your smear report says, 'No endocervical cells seen. Negative'? Should you have it repeated? I think the answer to this is yes, but not straight away. You should not panic that the smear is worthless. Bear in mind it is not proven that these cells make a difference. However, I do not think you should leave it three or five years before having a routine repeat smear. A repeat in a year seems sensible, just to be on the safe side.

CERVICAL ECTOPY OR EROSION

'I was lying on the couch and the nurse was just asking me about my daughter, her son goes to the same school, when she suddenly said, "Oh, you've got an erosion." I nearly stopped breathing.'

This is another term which causes much unnecessary anxiety. It is a harmless appearance of the cervix, which is particularly common in young women, women who are pregnant, who have had children, or who are taking the combined oral contraceptive pill. Those categories include a lot of people.

It simply means that there are some soft, columnar cells on the outside surface of the cervix. Usually these cells stay inside the womb and the cervical canal. They have a good blood supply, so they appear red in colour. If they decide to move outwards, their red colour gives the surface of the cervix a grazed look, which is why it was originally called an erosion. Actually, nothing is being 'eroded', so the word is inaccurate as well as rather frightening. For this reason we now call the appearance ectopy, or ectropion, derived from the Greek words meaning eversion, or turned inside out. It is quite harmless, but it can become a nuisance.

If an ectropion is large, you may notice more discharge than before. The discharge will be odourless and non-itchy, just like normal discharge. You may also notice some light bleeding after intercourse. This is because the columnar cells are well supplied with blood vessels (causing bleeding) and glands (which produce discharge).

If the discharge or bleeding become a nuisance, it is quite simple to have the ectropion treated. This is usually done by freezing the area, a procedure called cryotherapy (*kryos* means frost in Greek). The treatment is done in an outpatient clinic and is very quick. A small, very cold metal instrument is pressed on to the cervix for a couple of minutes; you won't feel anything much at the time, though you may get some period-type pain. It is often a good idea to take a couple of painkillers beforehand just in case. Afterwards you are likely to have some discharge for several weeks, which is just the healing process. In fact, the discharge afterwards is by far the most tiresome part of the treatment and is the main reason for not treating an ectropion unless it is actually giving you problems. Sometimes the ectropion may gradually come back because the conditions that led to it are still there – another reason for not treating unless it is really bothersome.

CANDIDA (THRUSH)

Candida is an extremely common infection, which happens to show up on a smear, but is not in any way related to cervical abnormalities. In fact, it could be argued that it is not really an infection at all, since candida is present normally in the vagina.

Candida, also popularly called thrush or yeast infection, is a fungus. It is a normal inhabitant of both the bowel and the vagina. Given half a chance it will multiply and occupy more and more space, resulting in a creamy, curd-like discharge. Indeed, this discharge led to its name, since *candidus* means white in Latin. The

22 Cytological pattern		23 Specific infection		24 Management suggested	
inadequate specimen	1	trichomonas	1	normal recall	1
negative	2	candida	2	repeat smear in ____ months	2
borderline changes	8	wart virus	3	or after treatment	3
mild dyskaryosis	3	herpes	4		
moderate dyskaryosis	7	actinomyces	5	gynaecological referral	4
severe dyskaryosis	4	other (specify)	6	cancel recall	5
severe dyskaryosis/ ? invasive carcinoma	5	Signature		date	
? glandular neoplasia	6				

Smear form showing candida

other thing you may notice is itching, often very
intense, around the outside, the vulva. In many cases,
however, there are no symptoms and candida simply
shows up on testing either on an infection swab, or on
a smear. Its other medical name, monilia, is derived
from its bead-like appearance under the microscope
(*monile* means necklace in Latin).

The vagina is also normally inhabited by a number of
bacteria: not all bacteria are bad for you, some are
positively helpful. One particularly good type is the
lactobacillus, which produces lactic acid. This creates
an acidic environment in the vagina, which candida
doesn't like very much. So it sits around, curled up in
a corner, waiting for conditions to improve.

Anything which reduces the acidity of the vagina will
help candida to grow. If you are given a course of
antibiotics for an ear infection, those antibiotics will
certainly kill off the nasty bacteria in your ear. Unfortunately, at the same time they will also wipe out nice
lactobacillus. Candida suddenly wakes up: no acid!
Antibiotics work only on bacteria, not fungi, so they
will leave candida untouched and multiplying furi-
ously.

If you are very run down or have the flu or some
other illness, your immune system will be busy fighting
that and will have less time to think about candida.
Again, under these circumstances, attacks of thrush are
more likely.

You can also reduce the acidity of your vagina by
using perfumed bubble baths and soaps, as they are
very alkaline. In some women, this will be enough to
allow candida to multiply. Of course, if you are already
suffering from an attack of thrush, you will make
things very much worse if you then use such products.
Biological washing powder will also make things

worse, by attacking already sensitive skin.

Candida loves the tropics. Heat and humidity are its favourite types of weather. In such conditions, or at any time if you are prone to thrush, you will find stockings better than tights and cotton underwear better than nylon.

Candida is very common in pregnancy, which is probably a combination of the immune system being somewhat depressed and the hormonal changes that are occurring. Nearly everyone thinks thrush is more common in women on the combined oral contraceptive pill, but scientific studies have not confirmed this. A great many women take the pill and a great many women get thrush: there is bound to be an overlap, which in the majority of cases is just coincidence.

Although candida is a normal inhabitant of the bowel, it may spread from there in large numbers into the vagina. This will help the vaginal thrush win its battle against lactobacillus (reinforcements!). Wiping backwards, not forwards, after a bowel motion will help prevent this happening. If the problem is recurrent and persistent, it is sometimes worth taking a course of anti-fungal tablets (usually nystatin, or, a newer treatment, Diflucan), to try to reduce the bowel candida population.

Vaginal thrush can make you feel as though you have cystitis, with irritation and burning when you pass urine. Unlike 'real' cystitis, bacteria will not be found in a urine sample sent for culture: the effect is local, at the entrance/exit of the urethra, rather than caused by an actual bladder infection.

The treatment for thrush is usually a course of pessaries (which look like suppositories) and cream. The pessaries are put into the vagina at night, and the cream spread round the outside (the vulva) twice a day.

You can buy treatment over the counter at the chemist, in the form of Canesten 1 (a strong pessary – only one is needed) and Canesten cream. It is often worth sharing a little of the cream with your partner: although candida is not a sexually transmitted disease, spores can travel backwards and forwards.

There is a newer treatment for thrush, which many women prefer as it only requires swallowing one tablet, called Diflucan. This is just as effective as the pessaries and creams, without the mess. However, it is no better at preventing recurrences.

Some women (fortunately a small minority) have real problems with recurrent candida infection. It can make life very miserable if it keeps coming back every few weeks. In such cases, the best strategy is scrupulously to avoid all the things that make its life easier: the bubble baths, soaps, biological washing powder and so on.

Recurrent attacks are often prevented by using a pessary (such as Canesten 1) once a week, whether or not you have symptoms, to try to keep the candida population down. Sometimes it is advised that you also use a pessary after having sex.

However, if you do have recurrent attacks of thrush, you would be best getting advice from a sexually transmitted disease clinic (also called departments of genito-urinary medicine or 'special' clinics). They have the most expertise at dealing with all vaginal infections, whether sexually transmitted or not. In addition, if the discharge is not going away with normal candida treatments, it may not be thrush at all, but something else. Many discharges are itchy, but may not be due to thrush. These clinics will do the swab tests for you and will be able to give you at least part of the answer the same day.

GARDNERELLA

Gardnerella, also called anaerobic or bacterial vaginosis, is another very common infection, this time caused by a bacterium. It should not be confused with the much more serious gonorrhoea, to which it is not in any way related.

Like candida, gardnerella is a normal inhabitant of the vagina and is usually not noticed at all. However, if it is present in large numbers, it can cause a discharge, which is not likely to be itchy but may smell slightly fishy, especially after intercourse.

'Clue cells', which may be mentioned on a smear report, are normal cells to which the bacteria attach themselves. Together, they have a characteristic appearance under the microscope, giving a 'clue' that

21 CYTOLOGY REPORT

Clue cells suggestive of gardnerella

22 Cytological pattern		23 Specific infection		24 Management suggested	
inadequate specimen	1	trichomonas	1		
negative	2	candida	2	normal recall	1
borderline changes	8	wart virus	3	repeat smear in ___ months	2
mild dyskaryosis	3	herpes	4	or after treatment	3
moderate dyskaryosis	7	actinomyces	5	gynaecological referral	4
severe dyskaryosis	4	other (specify)	6	cancel recall	5
severe dyskaryosis/ ? invasive carcinoma	5	**Signature**		**date**	
? glandular neoplasia	6				

Smear form result showing gardnerella

gardnerella may be present. They are not related to cervical abnormalities.

This condition is currently the subject of intense debate. Until recently, most doctors would treat a woman only if she actually complained of a smelly discharge, as it was thought to be quite harmless. However, there is now a suggestion that anaerobic vaginosis may play a part in pelvic inflammatory disease (PID or salpingitis), which can result in infertility. In addition, it has been linked with an increased risk of premature babies. It has not actually been proven to cause either of these problems, but doctors are becoming interested in its possible role. Thus, the current tide of opinion is in favour of treatment with or without symptoms. But do you treat the partner for a condition which probably isn't sexually transmitted? Well, opinions are greatly divided on this: my view is that if you are going to treat a woman, you might as well treat her partner in case it goes backwards and forwards between them, just like thrush. But it is very important that everyone concerned (and in particular the couple) understand that it is just a precaution and no one is laying blame at anyone's door. To have a row over something as uninteresting as gardnerella would really be a shame.

Two types of treatment are now available. The well-established method is a five-day course of an antibiotic called metronidazole or Flagyl, 400 milligrams twice a day. Metronidazole tastes disgusting (I believe Flagyl is the more palatable version as it comes in capsules) and you can't drink any alcohol while you are taking it: if you do you will be quite unbelievably sick. The very unpleasantness of the treatment was one of the reasons why both doctors and their patients wondered if it was worthwhile.

A newer treatment is clindamycin (Dalacin) cream which is inserted into the vagina at night using an applicator. It should be used for seven days. Although it may be a little messy, at least it has fewer side effects and it appears to be as effective as metronidazole.

Of course, if you are being treated, you should not have sex until you have (both) finished the course, or you may just pass it back again.

TRICHOMONAS

Trichomonas vaginalis is a one-celled organism of a type known as a protozoan (in Greek, *proto* means first and *zoion* means animal – in other words, a very primitive animal). Trichomonas is fascinating to look at under the microscope because it swims around, moving its hairs, or flagellae (so called because this is the Latin for whip, describing their whip-like motion).

As you can see from the illustration on page 52, Trichomonas is pear-shaped, with the flagellae at one end. It swims its way into your vagina during sex, though it is *just* possible to catch it from swimming

22 Cytological pattern		23 Specific infection		24 Management suggested	
inadequate specimen	1	trichomonas	(1)		
negative	2	candida	2	normal recall	1
borderline changes	8	wart virus	3	repeat smear in ___ months	2
mild dyskaryosis	3	herpes	4	or after treatment	3
moderate dyskaryosis	7	actinomyces	5	gynaecological referral	4
severe dyskaryosis	4	other (specify)	6	cancel recall	5
severe dyskaryosis/ ? invasive carcinoma	5	Signature		date	
? glandular neoplasia	6				

Smear form result showing trichomonas

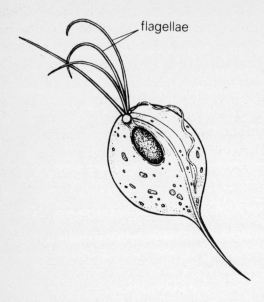

Trichomonas vaginalis

pools or lavatory seats. Men usually have no symptoms and so do not realise they are passing it on. In fact, tests for infection may not even show it up in a man. However, although some women also have no symptoms, many get a nasty, frothy, itchy discharge, which smells of old fish. As with candida, the local irritation can make you feel as though you have cystitis.

Because of the intense inflammation it causes in the vagina and cervix, you can have bleeding after intercourse. The inflammation, and the physical presence of these relatively large organisms, can make it difficult to interpret a smear, so you may be asked to have a repeat smear after you have been treated. Although trichomonas can 'spoil' your smear, it does not cause abnormal cells to develop.

The treatment for trichomonas is actually the same

as the traditional one for gardnerella, though the conditions are not related. You – and definitely also your partner – have to take a five-day course of the antibiotic metronidazole (Flagyl), 400 milligrams twice a day (Dalacin cream has not been shown to be effective against trichomonas). Obviously, you must not have sex during this time, or you will reinfect each other. You must also not drink alcohol while taking metronidazole, or you will be very sick.

Unfortunately, trichomonas likes company. It is quite often the case that if you have been infected with it, you will find you have another infection as well. So it is always advisable to be tested at a genito-urinary medicine (sexually transmitted disease) clinic, to be sure there is nothing else there.

ACTINOMYCES-LIKE ORGANISMS

Actinomyces is a bacterium which, once again, is a normal inhabitant of the bowel. However, in women who use an intrauterine contraceptive device (IUD), it very occasionally migrates into the vagina. This seems to be more likely when the IUD is the older, plastic, rather than copper-containing, type. Because of its rarity and the fact that it cannot absolutely reliably be diagnosed on a smear, cytologists will usually say they have seen actinomyces-like organisms (ALOs) rather than actual actinomyces. Actinomyces does not cause abnormal cells, it is being reported just for information.

Unfortunately, *very rarely* actinomyces can cause a potentially serious type of pelvic inflammatory disease (PID or salpingitis), which can lead to problems, including infertility as a result of blocked Fallopian tubes. Thus, if your smear does show ALOs, your

21 CYTOLOGY REPORT

Actinomyces - like organisms
seen

22 Cytological pattern		23 Specific infection		24 Management suggested	
inadequate specimen	1	trichomonas	1	normal recall	1
negative	2	candida	2	repeat smear in ___ months	2
borderline changes	8	wart virus	3	or after treatment	3
mild dyskaryosis	3	herpes	4		
moderate dyskaryosis	7	actinomyces	(5)	gynaecological referral	4
severe dyskaryosis	4	other (specify)	6	cancel recall	5
severe dyskaryosis/ ? invasive carcinoma	5	Signature		date	
? glandular neoplasia	6				

Smear form showing that actinomyces-like organisms have been seen

doctor will ask whether you have noticed any pain or discharge. You will be examined for signs that you need treatment. If there are no signs, you could just watch and wait, having annual cervical smears, given that the number of cases of actual PID due to this organism is so small. You would have to be particularly careful to seek advice if you had even the slightest twinge of pain or discharge. Many women cannot tolerate this kind of uncertainty and choose the other option, which is the one I would normally recommend. This is to have the current IUD removed and replaced immediately with another one. The new IUD should be a copper-containing one. Once this is done, a cervical smear taken six months later is almost always clear of the ALOs.

SEVERE INFLAMMATORY CHANGES –
THE INFLAMMATORY SMEAR

I sincerely hope you will never see this term on a smear form. Indeed, I hope that I will never again see it on a smear report either. What does it mean? Don't ask me. In fact, don't ask anyone: nobody knows.

I'm not being funny. The category has been removed from the new smear form in an effort to try to stop cytologists using it. If used, it means completely different things to different people.

To some, inflammatory changes mean that there is an infection of some kind present, but they can't see anything specific (such as candida or trichomonas). They can see a lot of white cells, which are pus cells, arriving to combat infection. The cervical cells themselves may also be showing some signs of battle against infection. You need to have a check-up for infection and have your smear repeated afterwards (in practice the repeat smear is usually done six months later).

However, to others, 'severe inflammation' means the cells are showing minor changes, not enough to call the condition 'mild dyskaryosis' but not normal either. Borderline abnormal cells, in fact. In this case, there may or may not be an infection present, but the important thing is that the cells are not quite normal. You will notice on page 56 that the new smear form has included a category called 'borderline changes' to try to force the cytologist to make a decision. In the past, when the category 'severe inflammatory change' was available, there was a temptation to throw into it anything that the cytologist wasn't quite sure of. 'Can I call this normal? Maybe the cells look a little abnormal. Maybe not. Oh, I'll call it severe inflammatory change to be on the safe side.' But it wasn't safe at

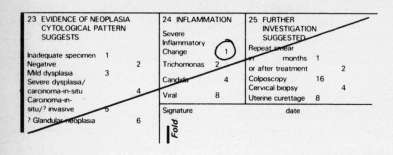

Old smear form

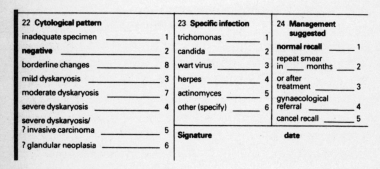

New smear form

all, because no one knew what it meant, so it was often ignored.

Of course, two problems can occur at the same time. If there is an infection, sometimes it is hard to distinguish the appearance of the cells from a borderline abnormality. This may happen with both candida and trichomonas, but then usually these infections will also be seen and the smear can simply be repeated after they have been treated.

Some laboratories hedge their bets by using a category they have introduced for themselves called 'inflammatory bordering dyskaryosis'. In effect, that again means, 'Maybe there's an infection there, maybe there isn't. Maybe the cells are a little abnormal, maybe they're not.' In this case, the chances are you will be asked to have a check-up for infection and a repeat smear in six months – that covers every eventuality. In practice, since infections such as thrush are very common, there is a high chance that some kind of infection will be found. However, there is a lack of good studies which compare women who have inflammatory/borderline smears with women who are otherwise similar but have normal smears. Some studies show that in both groups a similar percentage of women will have some kind of infection, others show that those with inflammatory/borderline smears are more likely to have an infection. Of course, they don't always use the same criteria for defining their inflammatory/borderline smear reports . . .

It is still a bit of a mess. Indeed, this area highlights one of the disadvantages of a screening test which relies on a subjective assessment of what cells look like: they look different to different people, and may even look different to the same person on a different day.

A smear reported properly as 'borderline change' is usually repeated after six months. If it is again abnormal, you may be asked to have a colposcopy (see Chapter 4), or you may have the smear repeated yet again, six months later. This will vary according to the area in which you live and the facilities available.

If your smear repeatedly shows borderline (or 'inflammatory/borderline') changes, you should have a colposcopy. It is reasonable to repeat the smear once, perhaps even twice, provided that the tests are not more than six months apart. Thus, at worst, you will have a colposcopy within a year of your first borderline abnormal smear. Studies have shown that in up to 30 per cent of cases where there is a persistent borderline abnormality, there will be CIN present, of varying degrees of severity.

There is another reason why cells may look slightly abnormal. If you have gone past the menopause, your body stops producing the hormone oestrogen. This may make your vagina feel dry and the skin lining it (and everywhere else in your body) thin. These changes are called atrophic changes from the Greek *trophe*, meaning nourishment, and the prefix *a*, which means without. Cervical cells may also look atrophic, and they can then be difficult to distinguish from a border-line abnormality. In this case, it is often worth trying a short (six-week) course of vaginal oestrogen cream and then repeating the smear. If lack of oestrogen was the cause, the repeat smear is likely to be normal. If it is not, you should be referred for colposcopy.

4

Having a colposcopy examination

'I think the worst part was waiting an hour to be seen. I was getting more and more nervous all the time.'

'In some ways, it helped seeing other women who all had the same problem as myself. I started chatting to the person sitting next to me and found we live quite near each other. She wasn't so worried, as she'd had it all done before and was just coming back for a check-up. She made me feel a lot better.'

Things have been improving in many colposcopy clinics, and the days of block booking everyone for the same time at the beginning of the clinic are over (I sincerely hope). Nevertheless, it is still likely you will have to wait to be seen. The chances are you will be anxious, even if you've been pretty level-headed so far. If possible, bring a friend or partner with you so that you have someone to talk to while you are waiting. That person may also be very useful when you are seeing the doctor: you may be so nervous that afterwards you cannot remember much of what was said. Or you may find it difficult to ask questions, and your friend or partner can prompt you, or ask them for you.

You may be asked to change into a gown. Frankly, I have never seen the point of this. If you are wearing a loose skirt, all you need to do is take your panties and tights off once you are inside the examination room. Trousers and tight skirts are not a good idea as they definitely will have to come off, in which case you may want a gown to make yourself feel less exposed during the examination.

> '*I wanted to ask so many questions. But when I was in with the doctor I couldn't think of them, I was nervous and muddled.*'

You may find it helpful to prepare a list of questions at home, in case they go out of your mind once you arrive. One thing you can definitely think about before you see the doctor is the date of your last period: I *guarantee* you will be asked. This is the single greatest time-wasting procedure I can think of. For the tenth time that day, I ask, 'When was your last period?' and suddenly there is a panic-stricken face in front of me. 'Oh, I think it was last month. I've got my diary here somewhere, just a minute. Erm ... oh dear, I don't seem to have noted it down. No – here it is, the 27th.' Although it is sometimes nice to vegetate for a few minutes while this is going on, wouldn't you rather I, or whoever you are seeing, was using that time to answer some of your questions?

> '*I had a lot of things I wanted to ask. But there were so many people waiting, I felt I would be taking up too much time. The doctor was so busy.*'

Of course, if no one opened their mouth except to say the date of their last period, clinics would be over in a fraction of the time. But although the doctors and nurses are busy, they are there to look after you, and that includes answering your questions. Don't be put off; after all, how often do you get the opportunity to talk to an expert about what is wrong with you? Books, leaflets and friends are all very well for general information and advice, but you will only be able to find out what specifically applies to you from the doctor doing the examination.

The doctor will also ask you some questions relating to your periods, your method of contraception, whether or not you smoke and your general medical history. This does not usually take very long: most of the discussion will be about your smear and what it all means. Bear in mind that some of the answers to your questions can only be given after the examination has taken place and the doctor has had a look at the area of abnormality.

THE EXAMINATION

Lurking in the background, you will notice a funny-looking couch, angled slightly. The bottom end is missing and instead it will have leg rests or stirrups. You will be asked to lie down on it so that your bottom is right at the end of the couch. Depending on the type of couch, your knees will be lying on top of knee rests, or in stirrups, or they will be bent and your feet positioned in foot rests. No matter how it is done it is very inelegant, but this position makes it easier to see your cervix. (The womb is actually quite mobile and will change its angle according to your position.) Indeed, in many other countries, women also have their

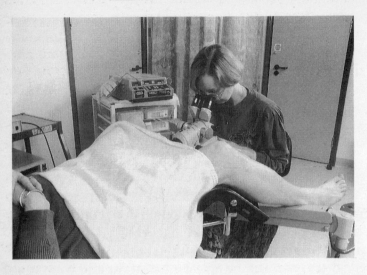

Colposcopy examination

smears taken lying on this type of couch. I am always having to stop bewildered American ladies shuffling down to the end of our conventional clinic couches, trying to find the stirrups.

> 'It was really good having the nurse there. She was very friendly and chatted to me, even held my hand while I was having the biopsy. Actually, it wasn't so bad, but it made me feel better, that she was there.'

Some clinics now have video equipment so that you can watch your own examination taking place. Not everyone likes this, so don't feel intimidated, you can always ask to have it switched off. Sometimes there are pictures on the ceiling or on an adjacent wall to keep your mind occupied. There may even be soft music. I have seen women bring a personal stereo along: if you do this you can listen to music of your own choice. All clinics have nurses who will do their best to put you at your ease and make you feel comfortable.

> '*It was horrible. Suddenly, there was a crowd of people standing at the end of the couch, all looking at me. I think they were students. The doctor seemed more interested in talking to them than to me.*'

Unfortunately, colposcopy has to be taught to other doctors, and the only way to learn is by practical training. However, you should never have to put up with the sort of experience described above. For a start, you have the right to refuse any other doctor or student being in the room. Indeed, the doctor should ask for your permission to have another person there, not just herd strangers in. And it is very intimidating to have several other people there: one extra is enough.

I have also seen clinics where doctors and students walk in and out of rooms while women are being examined. There you are, nether regions exposed, while strange men suddenly appear. They may know they are doctors, but as far as you are concerned they could be Joe Bloggs. This type of behaviour should be on the way out, but one way of preventing it is to ask for the door to be locked while you are being examined.

Anyway, you are lying comfortably on a couch, I hope, perhaps listening to soothing music and gazing at an interesting picture. There will now be some fumbling around while the doctor gets the colposcope into position. Although it is quite a large, intimidating instrument, all it comprises is a magnifying glass and a light source. The light illuminates your cervix and the magnifying glass enables the doctor to see what is going on. It is that simple.

No part of the colposcope enters you. Instead, a speculum (hopefully warmed) is inserted into your vagina, just as for a smear. However, this speculum will stay in longer than for a smear, usually about five minutes. Again, as with smears, the more you can relax the less uncomfortable the procedure will be.

Your cervix will then be wiped with some cotton wool soaked in dilute acetic acid. Acetic acid is the technical term for vinegar, and indeed, you may detect the familiar smell in the room. The acetic acid may sting a little and feel cold, but it doesn't hurt. For reasons we do not yet fully understand, acetic acid stains abnormal areas white, and the degree of whiteness is one of the features which help the doctor decide the degree of abnormality. It takes a little time for the white areas to show up, so at this point you will probably find yourself discussing the weather, your job, where you are going on holiday...

Sometimes the doctor will then also put some iodine on your cervix, again using a cotton swab. This is another way of showing up abnormal areas: they do not go dark brown as you would expect; instead they stay pale yellow. Because the contrast between dark brown/pale yellow is greater than that between white/pink, iodine is a good way of 'double checking' that no abnormal area has been missed. It also makes it easier to see the size of the area. If iodine is used, you will get a dark brown discharge for a couple of days.

If there is an abnormal-looking area on your cervix, the doctor will take a tiny piece from it called a punch biopsy. The biopsy is about the size of a pin-head and you could liken the procedure to having a cut on your finger. Many women are unaware anything has happened, others feel a short, sharp pain. However, most women do have a mild period pain afterwards and some feel a little sick, as you can when you are having period pain. To prevent this, it may be helpful to take a painkiller beforehand – preferably about fifteen to twenty minutes in advance, to give it time to work. There is a painkiller designed for period pain, called Ponstan (mefenamic acid), which is often good in this situation; unfortunately it is only available on prescription. A more easily available alternative is Neurofen (ibuprofen), which you can buy over the counter at the chemist. It will not make you drowsy, but it is related to aspirin, so it is best taken with some food, or it can upset your stomach.

You are likely to have some bleeding after a biopsy, just as you would if you cut your finger, so a tampon is often put in for you before the speculum is removed. At last the whole thing is over; you will probably be surprised to find how quick it really was.

A WORD ABOUT 'ACETOWHITE CHANGE'

Much of the technique of colposcopy is based on the white appearance which occurs when dilute acetic acid is wiped across the cervix. This phenomenon was first described in the 1930s and the procedure adopted with enthusiasm – but without understanding why it happens. At first, doctors thought that everything which became white was abnormal, but it is now known that this is not the case. Although abnormal areas do turn white, the same thing will happen in a number of normal conditions. For example, areas of cells undergoing the normal process of squamous metaplasia (see pages 23–6) will turn white. In fact, cells involved in any kind of change, normal or abnormal, seem to go white.

In recent years, research has started to look at

acetowhite change and early results suggest that the appearance may be due to the presence of certain types of cytokeratins. These are molecules which protect cells: for example, keratin in the skin makes it water-proof and resistant to attack. The cervix is in a nicely protected environment and does not normally need the extra protection of cytokeratins. However, studies of biopsies taken from areas showing acetowhite change show a lot of certain types of cytokeratin, in contrast to biopsies taken from areas which are not acetowhite. Perhaps cells which are in the process of change and are feeling vulnerable, or are already under attack, 'call in' cytokeratins for protection, resulting in the familiar white appearance.

Why am I boring you with all this extremely technical detail? Just so that you understand a very important and very simple concept: not everything which turns white with acetic acid is abnormal. False alarms can occur. (We will also be discussing this in relation to cervicography in Chapter 11.) I sometimes see women who are actually worried when I tell them the good news that their biopsy showed no abnormal cells. 'But didn't you say you saw something that might be abnormal?' Well, now you can understand why that may be wrong.

AFTER THE EXAMINATION

The biopsy specimen is placed in a preservative solution (formalin) and sent away to a laboratory. There it will be studied very carefully under a microscope. The biopsy gives a more accurate result than a smear, which is not really surprising: after all, a smear is just some loose cells, while a biopsy is a small but solid piece of tissue. Although abnormal cells look different individually, they are also arranged in different ways: in a mild abnormality, CIN 1, only one third of the cells above the basement membrane are abnormal. In CIN 2, two thirds of the cells are abnormal, while in CIN 3 all the cells are abnormal (see the illustration below). Obviously, you cannot see the extent of the abnormal cells if they are loose, you need a solid area, which is what is provided by a punch biopsy.

The results of the punch biopsy usually take a week or two to come back, though in very urgent cases the laboratory can manage to provide them within a couple of days. So, although the doctor who has examined you will be able to give you their impression of the degree of abnormality, you will not get a definite

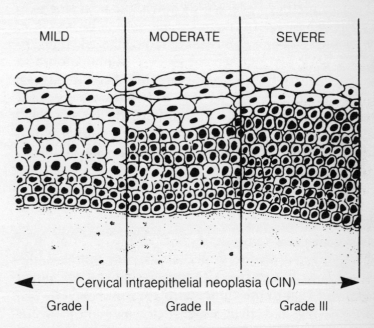

The changes on the cervical surface (CIN), as reported by the pathologist from the biopsies

answer on the same day. This is a shame, because waiting always involves anxiety, but there is no alternative. Usually, at least the doctor will have been able to reassure you that you do not have cancer, which for many women is the most important thing. It is more difficult to predict grades of CIN accurately; in addition, as mentioned above, not everything which stains white will actually turn out to be CIN. So you may find there is nothing wrong after all.

You may be made another appointment to come back for your biopsy result. Alternatively, you may be notified by post or sometimes by telephone. The procedure will depend on individual doctors and clinics.

Once the biopsy result is known, the next step is to decide what type of treatment, if any, will be best. You may not need any treatment, and may be asked just to come back for another colposcopy examination at a later date. If you do need treatment, there are several different kinds, which we shall be looking at in the next chapter. The type used in your particular case will depend on several factors: the degree of abnormality, the preference of the doctor, and what is available at the clinic.

'SEE AND TREAT' CLINICS

In recent years some clinics have offered the option of being treated on the same day as your initial colposcopy took place. The advantage is that you are spared an extra visit to the clinic; normally you would have a colposcopy and then come back another time for treatment, if the biopsy result confirmed that you needed it. This saves you time and obviously saves the clinic money, since they have to book you in only once.

Some women prefer this. If you are busy, taking time to come to the clinic can be a nuisance. Also, if you are treated straight away, you do not have to go on thinking about what might be wrong with you – it has already been removed.

There are two main disadvantages. The first is a medical one: you may be treated unnecessarily, because the result of the biopsy will not yet be known. The doctor may think you have CIN 2, but the biopsy may turn out to show only borderline changes, or may even be normal; in an ordinary clinic the result of the biopsy would have indicated that you did not need treatment, but in a 'See and Treat' clinic, the treatment will already have been done.

The second disadvantage, in my view, is that it can be too sudden. There you are, incredibly nervous, taking in only half of what is being said to you. You are only just beginning to understand what may be wrong – and you've been treated. Some women may prefer this, because they don't have time to panic about the treatment. But others may feel totally out of control. You have no time to go away and think about it, discuss it. You might have preferred the option of being monitored for a while to see if you got better without treatment – a reasonable thing to do if you have CIN 1.

As we will see in the next chapter, most treatments are now very quick and simple, so it is not the actual treatment that is a problem. But afterwards your activities will be restricted, so you may need to plan for this in advance (this is discussed in detail in Chapter 5). You may have planned a holiday in the next couple of weeks, it might be your anniversary, your partner has planned a surprise romantic weekend – and now suddenly you can't have intercourse. If you are going to a 'See and Treat' clinic, you should assume you are going to be treated and make all the arrangements, knowing they may have to be cancelled if you are not treated. And all this before you even know what is wrong with you!

The exception to this may be if you have had cervicography (see Chapter 11) following an abnormal smear and have already had a chance to discuss your worries and the various options in the clinic. Then you are likely to be more prepared and able to make decisions.

'See and Treat' clinics are very attractive to administrators because they save money, and they can save time for both doctors and women. But do not feel pressurised. You still have the option of saying you would rather wait for the biopsy result and come back, if you prefer.

UNSATISFACTORY COLPOSCOPY

Occasionally, a colposcopy examination may be considered technically unsatisfactory. This happens when the doctor sees an abnormal-looking area which stretches backwards into the cervical canal, but cannot see where it ends. Although what is visible may look mild, how can you be sure that the 'invisible' part isn't worse? The only way of finding out is to remove the abnormal area with a cone biopsy, described in the next chapter.

In this situation you will probably not have a conventional biopsy first, but will be made a separate appointment to come back for the treatment. The cone biopsy then provides both the piece of tissue that can be studied in the laboratory and the treatment at the same time.

A colposcopy may occasionally also be unsatis-

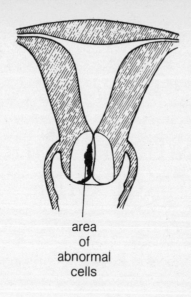

area
of
abnormal
cells

Abnormal-looking area extending high into the cervical canal

factory even if the doctor does not see anything that looks abnormal. You may have been referred with an abnormal smear, but the doctor cannot see the whole of the transformation zone (the area in which abnormal cells are most likely to occur). Everything visible looks normal, but again an abnormality in the 'invisible' area cannot be ruled out.

Having an unsatisfactory colposcopy does not mean anything sinister. It does not mean you are more likely to have cancer. It just means the position of your abnormal area (or your transformation zone) made it impossible to get a complete view at colposcopy. It is worth mentioning that the chances of this happening to you are very small: the vast majority of colposcopies are technically perfectly satisfactory.

5

Treatment options for CIN

The last ten years have seen great progress in the methods of treatment available for cervical abnormalities. The advent of colposcopy allowed the abnormal area to be properly assessed before treatment, but this would have been of limited use if the treatment options had not also improved.

This chapter will cover ways of treating cervical intra-epithelial neoplasia (CIN): the treatment of cancer will be discussed in the next chapter. There are now five treatment options available: cryotherapy, electrocautery, cold coagulation, laser treatment (which can either be a vaporisation or an excision) and loop diathermy. All of them aim to remove the abnormal cells, either by destroying them, or by cutting them out, while causing as little damage as possible to the surrounding normal tissues. The choice you are offered will depend to an extent on the preferences of your gynaecologist and on what is actually available at the hospital.

Since laser vaporisation and loop diathermy are now

the treatments most in favour I shall describe them first. These two treatments, although technically different, from your point of view are very similar. Both are done under local anaesthetic, take only a few minutes, require the same aftercare and have the same low frequency of long-term complications. First I shall explain the principles behind them.

LASER VAPORISATION

The word laser is derived from Light Amplification by Stimulated Emission of Radiation: the basic principle is that the laser machine produces a very fine, and therefore very concentrated and powerful, beam of light. Ordinary light 'sprays out', so its energy is lessened by being spread around more thinly. A laser machine manages to concentrate the light rays so that they stay in line: thus the energy is harnessed more effectively (see the illustration below).

This beam can then be moved around by means of

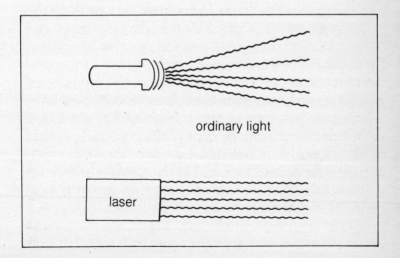

mirrors and lenses. In addition, the amount of energy it contains can be varied by changing the width of the beam: the narrower the beam, the more concentrated the energy.

As you know, light produces heat: think how hot a light bulb is if you touch it. The heat in a laser beam is so intense that it causes cells to evaporate into thin air. This is why the process is called 'laser vaporisation'.

If the beam is very fine, it will cut through cells like a knife; the laser can therefore also be used to remove pieces of tissue, as for a cone biopsy, which will be discussed later.

A laser machine needs to be attached physically to a colposcope, because it relies on the lens in the colposcope itself. This is a disadvantage, because only the more expensive types of colposcope can be attached to a laser. When you think that a laser machine itself costs around £30,000, if you then also have to use a colposcope costing over £10,000, the expense is considerable. (Ordinary colposcopes cost around £4000 to £5000.)

A laser machine looks like a large box, with a steel tube coming out for attachment to the colposcope (see the illustration opposite).

The light beam is conducted down the arm to the colposcope and is then directed on to the cervix using the lenses and mirrors in the colposcope. Although the beam itself is invisible, it is accompanied by a red light so that it can be seen. Because of the potential problem of the beam being reflected back into the faces of the doctor and nurse, they are likely to wear protective glasses. Indeed, although you are much less at risk, in some units you may also be offered glasses.

By looking through the colposcope, the doctor can guide the beam with great precision to ensure that only

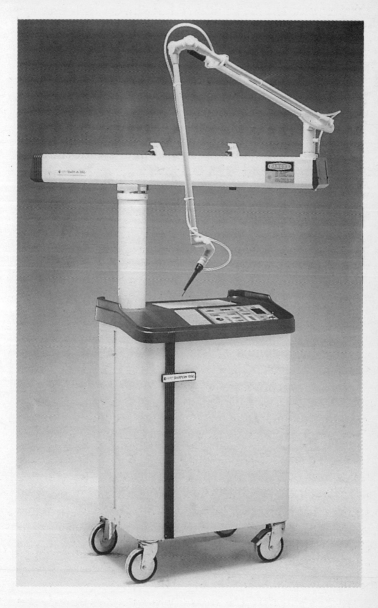

Laser machine

the abnormal tissue is removed, with very little damage
to the normal areas.

LOOP DIATHERMY

The correct name for this is Large Loop Excision of the
Transformation Zone, or LLETZ. Although the basic
idea of using hot wire loops to excise areas of the cervix
is not new, its introduction as a form of treatment dates
only from around 1987. However, it has rapidly
caught on and is taking over from the laser as the most
popular method of treatment.

The basic principle is that a thin wire heated elec-

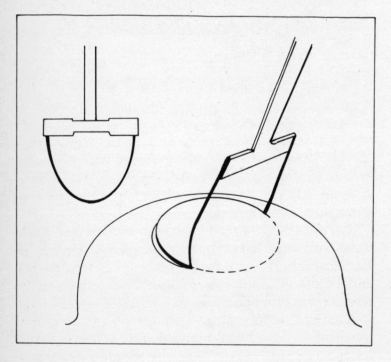

Loop diathermy in use

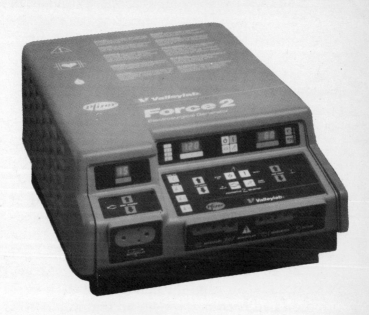

A loop diathermy machine

trically to a high temperature cuts through the cervical tissue rather like a cheese wire cuts through cheese. Because the wire is very thin and can be guided exactly by looking through the colposcope, the area excised is accurate and the damage to adjacent normal tissue is minimal, as with the laser.

One advantage of the loop method is that it is much cheaper than the laser. The machine which supplies the electrical energy is relatively cheap at between £4000 and £7000. In addition, it does not need to be directly connected to a colposcope, so a cheaper type is quite adequate. This has meant that the technique is not restricted to large, well-funded units, and brings the benefits previously associated with the laser to a wider public.

There is another advantage of the loop which has, in many experts' eyes, placed it ahead of laser vaporisation. Whereas the laser evaporates the cells away, never to be seen again, the loop preserves them, allowing the piece of cervix removed to be sent for examination in the pathology laboratory. This means that the whole abnormal area can be checked, not just the tiny area taken in a punch biopsy (see Chapter 4). Use of the loop has shown that punch biopsies are not always representative of the whole area: for example, a punch biopsy may show CIN 2 (the second stage of abnormal cells), but the loop specimen removed at treatment shows there is also some CIN 3. Occasionally, previously unsuspected early cancers have been found by examining the loop specimen: these had not been diagnosed by the doctor doing the colposcopy, and were not evident from the punch biopsy. If a laser vaporisation had been performed, no one would ever have known – until the woman developed problems if the cancer had not been completely removed by the treatment. This is another advantage of loop diathermy: when the piece of cervix is examined in the laboratory, the pathologist can tell if the whole abnormal area has been removed, because if it has, the edges of the piece will be free of abnormality. This is important information, especially for CIN 3, since, if some has been left behind, the doctor is alerted to arrange particularly careful follow-up. It does not, however, usually mean that you need another treatment straight away, as the abnormal cells left behind may yet be dealt with by your own immune system.

Although the loop has all these advantages, laser is still a perfectly viable option. The laser can also be used to remove pieces of tissue, by making the beam very fine, although this does take longer and is a little more difficult than with the loop. Small treatments performed in this way are called laser excisions, as opposed to cone biopsies which are larger (see page 89). If a doctor has become very good at using the laser for excision, the chances are you will not notice much difference. And some doctors are worried that the loop is too easy: it is tempting to overtreat, simply because it is such a simple procedure. Nevertheless, at present, the majority of experts are in favour of loop diathermy.

WHAT HAPPENS DURING A LASER OR LOOP DIATHERMY TREATMENT?

Both procedures are usually done in the outpatient clinic under local anaesthetic, unless there is a special reason why a general anaesthetic is necessary. This is sometimes the case if the area to be treated is very large, or if for some reason it is difficult for the doctor to have a good view of the cervix.

Most doctors prefer not to perform the treatment during the heavy days of a period, although light bleeding is not a problem. Heavy bleeding can obscure the view, making the procedure more difficult. You are also likely to bleed more heavily during and after the treatment because the cervix is already 'in the mood' for bleeding. If you are due a period when you are booked for treatment, it is worth phoning the clinic to check whether you should come.

'Having booked the childminder and got my mother organised to stay for the weekend, I suddenly realised I was going to have my period just at the time of the treatment. Typical. But, when I rang, the doctor said as I was on the pill, I could just run two

packets together to avoid having a bleed that month. She said it was quite safe to do that.'

Postponing a bleed is very easy if you are on the pill. The only exception is if you are taking a triphasic type of pill, which has three different doses in three different colours of pills. In this case, you would need to keep taking the last row of pills from other packets in order to maintain the same dose level.

Try to bring someone with you: although both types of treatment take only a few minutes, many women feel a little 'shaky' afterwards, often because they have been so anxious. It is nice then to have someone there, even better if they have a car in which to take you home.

You may be given some painkillers when you go in. These are usually Ponstan (mefenamic acid), designed to stop you having period-type cramps after the treatment. They are similar to Neurofen (ibuprofen) and are given at the start so they have time to work.

Since the first part of the procedure involves a colposcopy (see Chapter 4), the same principles apply: again, a loose skirt is a good idea, since you will not need to take it off. You will sit on the same type of couch as for a colposcopy, with your legs resting on foot rests or in stirrups. The doctor will do a colposcopy to locate the abnormal area, then he or she will put in the local anaesthetic. This is done in much the same way as at the dentist (except, of course, it is your cervix, not your gum, which is being injected!) and, indeed, many clinics actually use dental syringes and needles. Unfortunately, just as at the dentist, this can be the worst part of the procedure. Not everyone feels the injection, but some women do find it unpleasant. However, it is over quite quickly and then you should be numb for the treatment itself.

The local anaesthetic needs a few minutes to work, which is why you will find yourself discussing the weather, your job, the latest film releases and so on. When the doctor is ready to start the treatment, you will hear a hissing noise, which is a suction machine being switched on. This is attached by tubing to the speculum (the metal instrument in your vagina) and simply removes any unpleasant odour caused by the treatment.

If you are being treated by loop diathermy, a special pad will be stuck on to your thigh in order to 'earth' you: unfortunately this also provides a free leg-waxing treatment when it is removed.

> '*I was surprised at how quick the actual treatment was. Most of the time was spent talking beforehand and waiting for the anaesthetic to work. Once he started, I could hear a noise and I felt a bit hot inside once or twice, but it was over so fast. I didn't feel any pain and it can't have taken more than a couple of minutes.*'

Afterwards, you may be asked to lie down for a few minutes in another room, just to calm down and make sure there is no bleeding. It is at this time that some women feel a little faint – and we don't want you to keel over in the corridor! You may be given some antiseptic cream to put into your vagina at night. However, there is no evidence this really does protect against infection, so many doctors have now stopped advising its use. Remember to bring a sanitary towel with you, as not all clinics have them – and if they do, they may be non-adhesive and resemble nappies. Tampons are not suitable, as discussed below.

AFTER THE TREATMENT

You will need to go home and rest for the remainder of the day. Indeed, if possible, take the next day off as well. You will probably feel remarkably well, which is the biggest problem. Your cervix needs time to heal: there is a raw wound on which a clot is trying to form. Gravity is against it because whenever you stand up, your cervix is pointing downwards, so the clot may drop off. And if you do any heavy lifting, running, jumping, aerobics, horse riding, housework (yes, you finally have a medical excuse), it has no chance. You need to become a couch potato for a while. This is the time to watch all those videos, read lots of books and take up knitting.

Exercise of a different kind is also bad news: the last thing your cervix needs right now is to be hit. So no penetrative sexual intercourse for four weeks after the treatment, and for the four weeks after that, only with a condom. Remember raw wounds are prone to infection. For the same reason, no tampons and no swimming for the first four weeks. You will need to invest in 'Super Plus' sanitary towels (such a joy . . .).

It is quite normal, unfortunately, to bleed for up to four weeks after the treatment. The bleeding can take many forms: a watery discharge, spotting, or it may even resemble a period. It can stop for days, weeks even, and then start again at random. You are much more likely to bleed if you ignore the advice about taking it easy: the temptation is enormous because you will be feeling really well.

It is not advisable to go on long journeys or to holiday in remote places within the first four weeks: although you might think this is good time to go away, what will you do on a beach in the middle of nowhere if you suddenly start to bleed heavily and are worried?

If you do have heavy bleeding, the first thing to do is to put yourself to bed. Take some painkillers if you are getting cramps: Ponstan (mefenamic acid) or Neurofen (ibuprofen) are likely to be best, but paracetamol should also be adequate. In most cases, the bleeding will diminish if you rest. If you are very worried, call the hospital or clinic where you were treated: they will give you advice and may arrange to see you, occasionally even to admit you overnight. Obviously, if you are too far away from there, call your GP or go to the local hospital's accident and emergency department. If you go into hospital, the chances are you will simply lie in a bed there instead of at home. However, very occasionally the bleeding really is enough of a problem to warrant medical treatment, namely a stitch, or a cautery to seal the wound using the laser or the diathermy machine.

Although all these instructions and warnings may seem rather frightening, the vast majority of women have no problems at all and wonder what all the fuss was about. But, to say it again, don't be tempted to overdo it because you feel so well.

If you have an intrauterine contraceptive device (IUD)

'*I was stunned when the doctor said, "Oh, you've got a coil, that'll have to come out," and just whipped it out there and then. No one had said anything to me beforehand.*'

IUDs may need to be removed before the treatment as the threads can get cut off, making subsequent removal much more difficult. However, you do not want to be taken by surprise because you might become pregnant. IUDs work in retrospect, so if you have had otherwise unprotected sex in the week prior to removal, you could still become pregnant. The best thing to do is either to arrange an alternative method of contraception well before the treatment, or to use an additional method, such as the condom, for the week before.

FOLLOW-UP

Most clinics will arrange to see you for a colposcopy and smear between four and nine months after the treatment. If a smear is taken sooner than four (some doctors would now even say six) months after treatment it seems more likely to give a falsely abnormal result – this is because cells that are regenerating can be difficult to distinguish from cells that are abnormal.

Often one follow-up colposcopy is all you need: if everything is fine, you will then simply have yearly smears. However, if you were treated for CIN 3, or if there is any worry that some abnormal cells may have been left behind, it is likely you will be seen at least once more for colposcopy, just to be on the safe side. The timing and frequency of follow-up visits vary greatly from clinic to clinic, depending on an individual doctor's preference and the resources available.

What is the chance of the treatment failing?

There is a 90 to 95 per cent chance that you will require only one treatment, so the success rate is very good indeed. In general, the larger the area requiring treatment and the greater the degree of abnormality, the higher the chance that a second treatment may be required.

Are there any long-term problems?

'My friend had to have treatment some years ago and then she had two miscarriages one after the other when she tried for a baby. It took them three years before they managed to have Joe.'

When the only method of treatment was surgical, using a scalpel (knife), there was a risk of problems. A larger amount of tissue was removed than was really necessary, resulting in difficulties in becoming pregnant and also in a higher risk of miscarriage and premature babies. One of the great advantages of both these newer treatments is that there is very little risk of any of these problems; indeed, only about 1 per cent of women who have laser or loop diathermy are likely to have these difficulties.

OTHER FORMS OF TREATMENT

There are three other types of treatment, cryotherapy, cold coagulation and electrocautery. These are becoming less used now that laser and loop diathermy, which are more versatile, have become more popular. However, they are perfectly valid methods in certain circumstances.

The post-treatment instructions for all three methods are the same, and are similar to those following laser or loop diathermy, so, to avoid repetition, I shall give them here. Following all these treatments you are likely to have a watery, blood-stained discharge or frank bleeding for between four and six weeks. You will be asked to avoid penetrative sexual intercourse and the use of tampons for about the same length of time. It is also a good idea to avoid strenuous exercise for at least three weeks.

Cryotherapy

The word *kryos* means frost in Greek, and this method works by freezing the cells. The instrument used is called a cryoprobe and it is attached to a pressurised supply of carbon dioxide or nitrous oxide gas. When the pressure is released, the gas shoots down the inside of the metal rod up to the tip, making it very cold. (In fact, its temperature goes down to around minus 60 degrees Centigrade.) The tip of the cryoprobe is pressed on to the cervix and held there for about three minutes. One application (of only one or two minutes) is enough

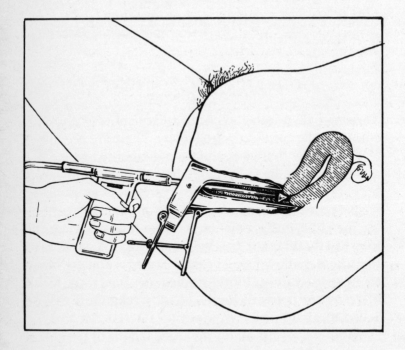

Applying the cryoprobe to the cervix

to treat a cervical ectopy (see page 43), but if CIN is being treated, the probe is removed for about five minutes before being reapplied for another three-minute dose.

Cryotherapy is a simple treatment, for which a local anaesthetic is not needed. However, you would be well advised to have some painkillers beforehand, as you are likely to feel a dull ache, or period-type cramps.

Because it is difficult to guarantee the depth – and the width – of treatment using cryotherapy, its use is limited to small areas of abnormality whose severity does not exceed CIN 2 (the second stage of abnormal cells). It is also used for the treatment of cervical ectopy. However, it can cause some scarring of the cervix, which may make follow-up more difficult. Its main advantages are that it is cheap, easy to do and does not require any anaesthetic.

Electrodiathermy

This should not be confused with loop diathermy, with which it has little in common. The principle is not too dissimilar from cryotherapy: an electrode is applied to the cervix, but this time heat is used, at 1000 degrees Centigrade.

Electrodiathermy has to be performed under general anaesthetic because it would otherwise be very painful. The electrode is held on until no more mucus is seen coming from the cervical glands. In this way, the depth of treatment is known to be adequate, even for areas of CIN 3: abnormal cells are very unlikely to extend below the level of the glands.

Although electrodiathermy is an effective treatment for all degrees of CIN, the fact that it has to be performed under a general anaesthetic makes it unattractive, especially compared with laser and loop diathermy treatments.

Cold coagulation

Although its name suggests a cold temperature, in fact this method uses heat: it is only 'cold' by comparison with electrodiathermy. This time a small probe is heated to 100 degrees Centigrade. It is applied to the cervix for 20-second intervals and the whole treatment only lasts a minute or two.

Cold coagulation does not require an anaesthetic and leaves no scarring. You may feel some dull, period-type pain during the treatment, so it is a good idea to take a couple of painkillers beforehand. This technique can be used for all grades of CIN.

IF YOU NEED A GENERAL ANAESTHETIC

Nowadays very few women need to have a general anaesthetic for treatment of cervical abnormalities. However, as mentioned earlier, if the area requiring treatment is particularly large or inaccessible, or if you are very nervous, a general anaesthetic may be advised. A general anaesthetic is also more likely to be advised if you need a cone biopsy (see page 89).

Many hospitals will now admit you as a day case, so you come in early, having not eaten or drunk anything since midnight. You will be seen by a junior doctor who will ask some questions and examine your chest, to make sure there is no danger in having the anaesthetic. If you have a chest infection or even just a cold it is unlikely they will go ahead and you will have to return another day.

'*The worst thing was the hanging around, waiting for things to happen. I was nervous and just couldn't concentrate on the book I'd brought. If I had to do it again I'd bring something really light, some magazines or a detective story or something. The woman in the next bed had just had her operation and was fast asleep, so I couldn't talk to her, but I had a chat with someone else who'd had my operation done two days ago. She seemed OK, which made me feel a bit better.*'

Just before you are taken into the operating theatre, you will be given a sedative injection or tablet. The next thing you know you will be waking up feeling groggy and perhaps a little sore. It is very important someone comes to collect you if you are going home the same day: you are unlikely to be fully 'with it' for several hours at least. And again, remember the sanitary towels.

If you have to stay overnight, the procedure is much the same, but is even more tedious since you are there longer. Most people find it hard to sleep in hospital wards; there is always noise, people walking around, telephones ringing. You may be offered a sleeping tablet; it is up to you whether to take it. If you are having a cone biopsy, you may have to stay in for a couple of days afterwards as well. Although you may think beforehand that you won't want visitors, I would advise you to have some, as you will be crawling up the wall with boredom before too long.

CONE BIOPSY

As its name suggests, a cone biopsy removes a cone-shaped piece of the cervix (see diagram on page 90).

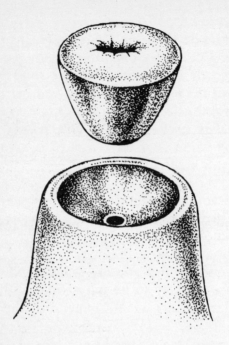

Cone biopsy

Before the introduction of colposcopy, this was the standard treatment for an abnormal smear: however, because in those days it involved a general anaesthetic and had long-term complications, only women whose smears persistently showed severe dyskaryosis were treated. Nowadays, it is performed only under these three circumstances:

1   If the abnormal area extends so far up into the cervical canal that its upper limit cannot be seen through the colposcope. The doctor may be quite happy that they can see no evidence of cancer, but what about the abnormal area which is not visible?

There is always the danger that something will be missed.

2   If a woman's smear keeps showing severe dyskary-osis but no abnormality can be seen on colposcopy to account for that result. Usually, if this happens, the doctor will repeat the smear first to make sure it was not a mistake: if it again shows severe dyskaryosis, a cone biopsy will be advised.

3   If, on colposcopy, the doctor is worried that the abnormal area may be starting to turn into an early cancer. In this case, the cone biopsy performs a dual function: by removing a relatively large piece of the cervix, hopefully it will remove all the abnormal area. In addition, as I discussed in the section on loop diathermy, the piece of tissue will be looked at very carefully in the laboratory to see exactly what was there, and whether the edges are clear of abnormality. In this way, the cone biopsy provides a diagnosis and, at the same time, the treatment.

The term 'cone biopsy' is really rather misleading as it is often confused with the tiny punch biopsy taken during colposcopy. Whereas a punch biopsy just gives information about what abnormality is present, a cone biopsy also, in most cases, will remove the abnormality as well. Thus, cone biopsy is really a form of treatment, which is why I have included it in this chapter.

Whereas the majority of women having a colposcopy will have a tiny punch biopsy taken, only around 10 per cent will need a cone biopsy.

There are now three possible ways of performing a cone biopsy: surgically ('knife' cone biopsy) or by using the laser or large loop diathermy.

Surgical ('knife') cone biopsy

If you are to have a surgical cone biopsy, you will need to stay in hospital for a few days. If you are due your period on the date booked, the surgeon may prefer to reschedule the operation, so it is worth ringing up to check.

The operation is short, lasting only about twenty minutes, but you will need to have a light general anaesthetic (see page 88). Usually, you come into hospital the day before the operation and stay for a couple of days afterwards. You are likely to have some period-type pain for a day or two and also to bleed for several days. Indeed, you may bleed on and off for several weeks after the operation: the post-treatment advice is the same as for laser or loop diathermy treatment (see pages 82–3).

Surgical cone biopsy can result in several problems. Firstly, the external cervical os (entrance to the cervical canal, see page 6) can become very tight afterwards. The technical term for this is 'stenosis' from the Greek word *stenos*, meaning narrow. If this happens, your periods may be painful and it may be very difficult to obtain an adequate cervical smear. By contrast, the internal cervical os may become too slack. This may occur if the cone biopsy had to be made long, because the area of abnormality was high up in the cervical canal (see opposite).

If the muscle of the internal os is damaged, there may be problems during pregnancy. The internal os stops the baby, which after all becomes heavier and heavier, from 'falling out' of the womb before a woman is ready to go into labour. If the muscle becomes weak, the weight of the baby may become too much for it and a miscarriage occurs. Most miscarriages occur early in

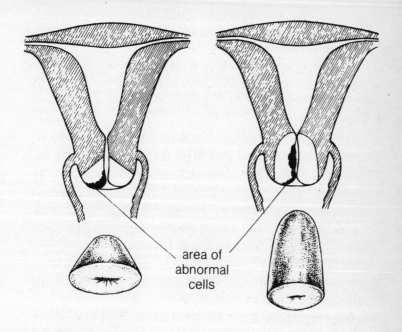

area of
abnormal
cells

a. 'Short' cone biopsy. *b. 'Long' cone biopsy*

pregnancy, but if weak muscle is the cause, the miscarriage will usually occur after the third month. In order to stop this happening, a stitch, which resembles a purse-string, can be inserted into the cervix during early pregnancy. This type of stitch is called a Shirodkar suture, after the doctor who first used it. It is removed when the woman reaches the thirty-eighth week of pregnancy and she then goes into labour normally. Incidentally, although problems can occur during pregnancy, having a cone biopsy is unlikely to cause any problems with fertility, that is, with your ability actually to become pregnant.

Surgical cone biopsies are smaller now than they were in the past because the area of abnormality can be mapped out more accurately using the colposcope. Because of this, the complications I have described are less likely to occur.

Cone biopsies performed using laser or loop diathermy

Both the laser and loop diathermy are now used to perform cone biopsies, and these have advantages over the surgical procedure. When a laser beam is made very narrow, the energy is so concentrated that the beam becomes equivalent to a knife: instead of just evaporating cells away, it will cut through tissue. Laser cone biopsies are more accurate and therefore remove less tissue than surgical cone biopsies. Because the laser beam is such a sharp, clean 'knife' and its heat helps blood vessels seal up quickly, there is less bleeding and less scarring than with surgical cone biopsies. As a result, they are much less likely to result in any of the problems described above.

The loop diathermy can be used for cone biopsies very simply by choosing a larger size wire loop. Otherwise the procedure is much the same as for an ordinary treatment. Indeed, with the advent of the loop diathermy, the whole distinction between ordinary treatment and cone biopsy has become slightly blurred: for example, if a woman has severe dyskaryosis on her smear, but nothing can be seen on colposcopy, nowadays it is possible to perform an ordinary loop treatment before resorting to a larger cone biopsy: if the specimen is found to have completely removed the abnormality, nothing further needs to be done. Like laser cones, the loop causes very little scarring and less tissue is removed than with surgical cone biopsies, so there are fewer long-term complications.

Both laser and loop diathermy cone biopsies can be performed under a local anaesthetic in the outpatient clinic, which is another advantage over the surgical procedure. However, the feasibility will depend on how large the cone biopsy needs to be, how easy it is to see your cervix and how nervous you are. They do take longer than ordinary treatments, so some women prefer a general anaesthetic. However, both types are less likely to cause problems with bleeding, so many women can go home the same day. Of course, all the advice given on pages 82–3 about your activities after treatment applies with even greater force under these circumstances.

WHAT HAPPENS AFTER A CONE BIOPSY?

The piece of your cervix is sent to a laboratory, where it is examined in detail. Your doctor will want to know not just what degree of abnormality was present, but also whether it has been completely removed, that is, whether the edges of the piece are clear of abnormal cells. The results usually take about two weeks to come through: some doctors ask you to come back to discuss them, or you may be notified by letter.

If there was no suggestion of early cancer, and the abnormality was completely removed, you will be seen usually four to nine months after the treatment, for a colposcopy and smear. Then, if everything is fine, you may be asked simply to have yearly smears, or the doctor may want to see you for colposcopy once more, again in six to twelve months, just to be on the safe side.

If the abnormality was not completely removed by the cone biopsy, you may be followed up more frequently in the colposcopy clinic, in case another treatment becomes necessary. Often, the remaining abnormal cells go away without further treatment, so it is worth watching and waiting for a while.

Another important part of the laboratory examination of the cone biopsy is to check whether it shows any signs of early cancer. Cancerous cells want to spread, so they push through the basement membrane, which normally keeps the outer layers of cells separated from the deeper tissues. The basement membrane has already been mentioned in Chapter 1 and I will go into greater detail about the spread of early cancer in Chapter 6. If the cancerous cells have spread only very slightly, the cancer is described as microinvasive: if it has been completely removed by the cone biopsy, no further treatment is likely to be needed, though obviously you will be monitored carefully. However, if there has been more extensive spread, further treatment will be required. All this is dealt with more fully in the next chapter.

AN ABNORMAL SMEAR IN PREGNANCY

Treatment is best avoided if at all possible during pregnancy. Even after a biopsy, bleeding can be a problem. Fortunately, the vast majority of abnormalities can safely be left for nine months, until the baby has been delivered. Remember that the cells take a long time to develop through all the stages of abnormality to actual cancer.

However, you will be monitored during the pregnancy and are likely to have at least one colposcopy (though biopsies are usually also avoided because of problems with bleeding) to check the area. In the vast majority of cases there are no problems.

What happens if you are found to have early cancer

while you are pregnant? This is always a difficult problem. There are many factors to be considered, including the degree of cancer and how far the pregnancy has progressed. Does the hospital, or one nearby, have good facilities for looking after premature babies? Each individual case is different.

> '*I just don't know what to do. I'm only eight weeks and the doctor says the safest thing would be for me to have a termination. But they want me to have a hysterectomy so this is my only chance of ever having a baby. Jim and I have wanted children so much, it would make us so happy to have just one. But what if the cancer spreads before I have the operation?*'

You will need to talk through all the options with your gynaecologist: ultimately, it is you and your partner who have to live with the consequences of any decision you reach, so you need to have thought about it very carefully.

WHY DO SOME WOMEN HAVE A HYSTERECTOMY WHEN THEY HAVE ONLY ABNORMAL CELLS, NOT CANCER?

Hysterectomy, or removal of the womb (uterus), is sometimes advised when there is another reason for doing it anyway. For example, if you also have very heavy periods, or fibroids (swellings of the muscle in the womb), and if you have completed your family, a hysterectomy would solve all the problems at once. Indeed, it would be pretty pointless to have treatment to your cervix, only to have the whole womb removed a few months later. However, a hysterectomy is a big operation, requiring a stay in hospital for a week, several weeks off work, and often two months for you to feel fully recovered. You should therefore have thought the decision through very carefully and discussed it thoroughly with your gynaecologist before going ahead.

If a woman has cervical cancer, her hysterectomy is likely to be performed in a different way to the 'normal' type. This will be discussed in the next chapter.

6

Cervical cancer and its treatment

So far in this book I have dealt with conditions (that is, abnormal cells) which, although they may have the potential to become cancer in the future, are in themselves quite harmless. In this chapter I shall look briefly at 'real' cervical cancer and how it is diagnosed and treated. In practice, a diagnosis of cervical cancer is rare in this country: at present around 4000 women each year develop it. This compares with between 200,000 and 300,000 women who have some kind of abnormality on their smear.

One of the difficulties in discussing cervical cancer is that every woman with cancer will have a different disease pattern, different circumstances and different individual considerations. Thus, the best person to ask for information and advice is your own gynaecologist, who knows the details of your case. Other people (even other doctors) and books can never give you specific advice and may actually be misleading.

Thus, this chapter is intended simply as a guide, to help you understand the basics. Then you should be better equipped to ask questions and make sense of the often quite complicated answers.

HOW WILL I KNOW IF I HAVE CERVICAL CANCER?

'I always thought you'd only need to go for a smear if there was something wrong. So when I started to get bleeding, often after we'd made love, I went to my doctor. He started to do the smear, but then said he'd send me straight to the hospital.'

'I just went along for my five-yearly smear. I'd never had any problems before. I guessed something was wrong because the doctor rang me to come and discuss my result.'

Unfortunately, you normally don't notice anything wrong until it is too late – or almost too late. This is why regular smears are important, even though everything feels fine.

There are a few signs to look out for, but all of these are more commonly due to something other than cancer. Unusual bleeding can be a warning sign, perhaps between periods, after sex, or suddenly for no reason after periods have completely stopped at the menopause. However, bleeding after sex is very often simply due to a cervical ectopy (see page 43), which is a harmless condition. Bleeding between periods can occur in women who use an intrauterine contraceptive device (IUD). Some women get a little spotting mid-cycle when they ovulate.

Women taking the combined oral contraceptive pill can have what is known as 'breakthrough bleeding', meaning bleeding on days when they are still taking pills. This can be caused by forgetting pills, taking interacting medication such as antibiotics, or having a stomach upset. If persistent, a change of brand should help. In any case of unusual bleeding, the doctor may first want to examine you and take a smear to be sure the cervix is normal.

Vaginal discharge may be a warning sign of cancer, but, of course, by far the most common reason is an infection. An ectopy can also sometimes cause discharge.

In the majority of cases of early cancer, women have not noticed anything unusual. The only way to prevent this happening to you is by regular screening.

SQUAMOUS CELL CANCER AND ADENOCARCINOMA

There are two types of cervical cancer. By far the most common, accounting for around 90 per cent of cases, is squamous cell cancer. This arises from the flat squamous cells, usually in the area of the transformation zone (see Chapter 1, page 8). When people talk about cervical cancer, this is the type they mean.

Adenocarcinoma ('carcinoma' is just another word for cancer) arises from the endocervical, columnar cells. It is rare; only around 10 per cent of cancers are of this type (and cervical cancer of any kind is not common in this country). It is much harder to detect by screening, as the cells are more difficult to pick up (they are more likely to be hidden inside the cervical canal) and also more difficult to recognise under the microscope. Indeed, screening is really designed to pick up the squamous cell abnormalities rather than these much, much rarer columnar cell ones. We still do not know a great deal about adenocarcinoma, either about its causes or its management. It may be on the increase, as the number of cases seems to be rising, but that may be partly due to the fact that doctors are becoming better at recognising it. It is still a grey area, and in this book I shall discuss squamous cell cancer in more detail, though the treatment for both types is similar.

HOW FAR HAS THE CANCER PROGRESSED?

Cervical cancer is described in terms of stages, or degrees of severity. These stages are useful for a couple of reasons. First, it means that different treatments can be compared fairly, since the chances of success are likely to be greater the earlier a cancer is found. Secondly, it means that a woman can be given a reasonable idea of what her chances are, based on experience of other women who have had cancer of similar severity.

I am not going to go into great depth about the staging, since it is quite complicated and involves a detailed knowledge of anatomy. In short, there are four stages, with each stage being further subdivided into two others, called a and b. The idea is to describe how far the cancer cells have spread. In a Stage 1 cancer, only the womb itself is involved. A Stage 2 cancer has spread just outside the womb, for example to involve part of the vagina. In Stage 3, the cancer is still contained within the pelvis, but only just. Stage 4 means the cancer cells have spread outside the pelvis, to the bladder, the bowel, or to more distant organs like the lungs and the liver.

How do cancer cells spread?

In very early cancer, the cells simply increase in number and push away or squash the normal cells. This is called microinvasion (see below). At this point it is still possible to remove the cancer cells by doing a cone biopsy (see pages 89–95), leaving the rest of the cervix and womb intact.

If the cancer cells are not stopped, they will carry on increasing in number and will eventually push their way into the lymph channels. Lymph is a liquid that carries immune cells (white cells) around the body. These immune cells are a little like policemen on the beat; there are always some around in the lymph channels, but if they sense intruders, such as bacteria, viruses or cancer cells, huge numbers will be alerted and rush to the scene.

Unfortunately, these lymph channels can also be used by cancer cells to spread themselves around the body. Lymph channels often run alongside blood vessels and constitute a large network, rather like streets in a city. Every now and again there are places where large numbers of immune cells congregate, called lymph nodes. You can think of these as police stations, containing large numbers of police, or immune cells. Cancer cells tend to get trapped inside lymph nodes, just as a criminal would find it hard to escape from a police station. However, they put up a fight, and so lymph nodes containing trapped cancer cells may be swollen and sometimes tender. You can now see why doctors often examine the lymph node areas: although you cannot see cancer cells moving, you can get an idea of whether they have spread by seeing if the lymph nodes have increased in size. (Incidentally, this swelling and tenderness of the lymph nodes can occur in any condition where the immune cells are fighting an intruder: infections are a much more common cause than cancer. So please do not panic if you unexpectedly find a slightly enlarged lymph node!)

By using lymph channels as if they were roads,

cervical cancer cells can gradually spread further and further away from their original site. Eventually they can reach organs as far away as the lungs. Obviously, the further they spread, the more difficult it is to get rid of them. Equally, if they have managed to get so far, they must have defeated the body's immune police, again reducing our chances of success.

For this reason, if there is any chance that the cancer has spread, tests need to be carried out to check where the cancerous cells might have reached. There is no point in taking out the womb if the lungs are already involved. Not all cancers behave in the same way: some appear to be more aggressive and spread faster than others.

MICROINVASION

As its name suggests, microinvasion is the very earliest stage of cancer, often referred to as 1a in the medical staging system.

If you recall the discussion of CIN change in Chapter 2, the important point about CIN is that it does not go through the basement membrane. It is wholly contained on the outside surface of the cervical 'skin'. When invasion starts to occur, the abnormal cells break through the basement membrane. In microinvasion, the cells can be seen to have only just broken through, and should not have managed to get far enough to reach the lymphatic channels. This is where problems start to occur, because it is difficult to be sure what depth of microinvasion is still 'safe'. If it is 'safe', then the cone biopsy – which is always done if there is a suspicion of microinvasion (see page 91) – will be enough to cure the condition. Otherwise, a hysterectomy will be necessary. This is why the cone biopsy is

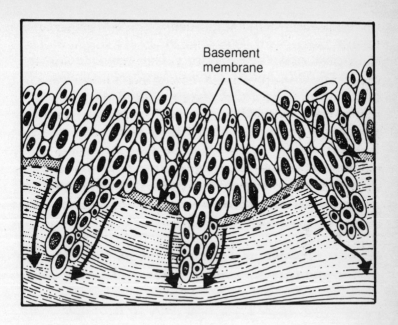

Abnormal cells crossing the basement membrane to the
connective tissue

looked at so carefully under the microscope: the
distance the cells have travelled on the 'wrong' side of
the basement membrane has to be measured to an
accuracy of less than a millimetre.

> '*John and I had only been married three months*
> *when the smear result came back, just showing*
> *abnormal cells. It was only when I went to the*
> *hospital that the consultant said I might have early*
> *cancer. It was such a shock. He said first of all I*
> *should have a cone-shaped piece removed and they*
> *would see if that was enough. So I had that done a*
> *week later. Actually, it wasn't as bad as I'd thought,*
> *it was all over in a few minutes. Waiting for the*

*result was the worst part. It took a week but it felt
like years. John went with me to the hospital. The
doctor said they probably had removed all the
cancer cells, but he couldn't be absolutely sure. He
asked if we wanted children. John and I hadn't
thought of starting a family quite yet, we had
thought we'd wait a couple of years. But we did
want children eventually. He said we should talk
about it, because it might be better to have a child
sooner and then perhaps have the hysterectomy for
my protection. He said we shouldn't decide there
and then, he'd see us again in a week.*

*We sat and talked all evening. At first John was so
worried about me that he said I should just have the
operation and we could always adopt a baby. But I
thought it would never be the same as having one of
our own. If we tried for a baby straight away, just
one, and then I had the hysterectomy afterwards, at
least we'd have a child, even if we did adopt a second
one. And, in the end, that's what we did. I've been
lucky: now I've got Amy and it seems I have been
cured. I still go for regular check-ups, but I feel
healthy. I think it's going to be OK.'*

Sometimes, even with all the careful measuring and
checking of the tissue, it is still not possible to be
absolutely sure that the lymph channels are clear. This
is one of the times when a woman's individual circumstances and wishes can influence what is done. If she
has completed her family and perhaps has other
gynaecological problems, she could opt for what would
be the safest course, which would be to have a
hysterectomy (removal of the uterus, or womb). However, she may have no children and still wish to have a
family. In this case, obviously, it would be very upset-

ting to have a hysterectomy. She may decide just to have the cone biopsy and be carefully monitored in the colposcopy clinic. This involves a slight risk, but one she may be prepared to take in order to be able to have children. As I said at the beginning of this chapter, in such circumstances, you need to discuss matters carefully with your gynaecologist.

INVASIVE CANCER

An obviously invasive cancer is more likely to cause symptoms such as bleeding and discharge. In this case, the cone biopsy will reveal that the cancer has spread through to the lymph channels, and therefore potentially to other areas of the body. For this reason, before any treatment is contemplated, tests need to be done to check the organs that might be involved.

The bladder, kidneys and rectum are close to the womb and are therefore obvious places to start. Often, the first thing the gynaecologist will want to do is a full internal examination under general anaesthetic. You may ask: why isn't the one he did while I was awake enough? The reason is that under anaesthetic your muscles are fully relaxed, which makes it easier to perform the examination and gives more information. In addition, the bladder can then be checked directly by having a flexible tube with a light source passed into it. This is called a cystoscopy and allows the doctor to see inside the bladder and check it for cancer. The same type of thing can be done for the rectum (back passage): not only can an ordinary examination be performed, but again, a special tube can be inserted to allow the doctor to see what is going on higher up.

The kidneys are checked by doing a special type of

X-ray called an intravenous pyelogram (IVP) or intravenous urogram (IVU). For this, you have a dye
injected into a vein in your arm. The dye travels
through the bloodstream to the kidneys and can then
be photographed while it is passing through the kidneys and bladder. Doctors know what the pictures
should look like if there is no abnormality, so they can
tell if there is something unusual there.

A chest X-ray is usually done to check there is no
cancer in the lungs – it is also useful if an operation is
being considered. You will have several blood tests, for
example, to make sure you are not anaemic.

Another test sometimes performed is a lymphangio-
gram. This shows up the lymph nodes and helps predict
which ones may have been invaded by the cancer. For
this, a special dye is injected into your feet: don't be
worried when you and your urine turn green, it does
wear off!

A number of other special scans and tests can be
done. Whether you have them will depend on whether
your gynaecologist feels they are necessary, and, of
course, whether they are available at your hospital.

When you have had these tests, your gynaecologist
will be in a position to discuss the treatment options with
you. Once again, what is done will obviously depend
partly on what he or she feels is the best form of
treatment, but also on what your own individual circumstances and wishes are. There are two main types of
treatment for cervical cancer: surgery and radiotherapy.
A combination of the two may also be used. In general,
doctors try to use surgery for younger women if possible,
since this usually allows the ovaries to continue functioning and has fewer long-term complications.

SURGICAL TREATMENT

This involves a special type of hysterectomy, called a Wertheim's hysterectomy. It is a bigger operation than a normal hysterectomy because the lymph nodes in the pelvic area are also removed. This is done for two reasons. First, removing the lymph nodes should catch cancer cells 'in transit' and stop them travelling onward. Secondly, the lymph nodes are looked at in detail under a microscope and, knowing where they came from, it is possible to tell how far the cancer has spread. This means the doctor can tell with more accuracy how successful the operation is likely to be.

Although the operation is a large one, the ovaries are left behind unless the woman has already gone through the menopause anyway. This is good for younger women, since it means they will still have functioning ovaries. However, there is a chance that the ovaries will gradually stop working anyway because their blood supply may have been slightly damaged during the operation. It is important to have blood tests to check the hormone levels occasionally, and especially if you notice hot flushes. If there are signs that the ovaries are running down, hormone replacement therapy can be given.

A Wertheim's hysterectomy is a long operation, often taking several hours. This is partly because of the time required to remove the lymph nodes, but also because it is all too easy to damage the bladder and other nearby organs if great care is not taken.

When you wake up, you will discover that you have a urinary catheter. This is a tube going into your bladder and attached to a bag, to keep your bladder empty. This is necessary because the bladder takes some time to start working properly again after the operation. You will stay in hospital for about two weeks, but most women find that it takes a couple of months before they feel completely back to normal.

By the time you leave hospital, the microscopic examination of the womb and the lymph nodes will have been done, so the doctor will be able to let you know those results and discuss what to do next, if anything. Often just having an operation is enough, but if many lymph nodes are found to contain cancer cells, a course of radiotherapy may be advised as well.

You will be followed up regularly every three months or so for the first couple of years and then gradually less frequently until you are seen just once a year. You may be asked not to have sex for the first couple of months after the operation to allow the area to heal.

Surgery is only possible while the cancer is still fairly early and therefore localised. As I mentioned earlier, it is preferable in young women because the ovaries are preserved and there are fewer long-term complications. However, if the cancer has spread beyond the pelvic area, thus being too advanced for surgery, or if surgical treatment is not successful in removing all of the cancer, radiotherapy may be better. This may also be the case in older women or those who for various reasons are not suitable for surgical treatment.

RADIOTHERAPY

Two types of radiotherapy can be used, internal and external. The cervix is unusual in that it is accessible enough for internal radiotherapy.

Internal radiotherapy involves inserting radioactive rods inside the vagina and uterus (womb). The advantage of this is that the cervix and uterus receive quite a high dose of radiation, but the bladder, bowel and rectum receive much less, because they are further away. This minimises the side effects of the treatment, described below.

Internal radiotherapy is a lonely procedure: you emit radiation while you are having it, so you have to be kept in a room on your own for a couple of days. However, you do not usually need more than three treatments, several days or even a week apart. The treatment itself does not hurt; most women complain more of boredom and being stiff from lying still.

Internal radiotherapy can be used on its own if the cancer is still fairly early, but the more advanced types require external treatment, to cover a larger area.

External radiotherapy involves short treatments spread over three to six weeks. It is rather like lying on a sunbed, and you can talk to the staff, who will be behind a protective screen. You usually have to come for the treatment several days each week, which is one of its most tiresome aspects. You need to keep travelling to and fro, all for a treatment which lasts a few minutes at a time. Since nausea and diarrhoea are common side effects, this travelling is not the trivial thing you would first suppose.

Internal and external radiotherapy are usually used in combination. External radiotherapy may also be used in combination with surgery, either to shrink the tumour before the operation, or afterwards, to clear any remaining cancer away.

During either type of radiotherapy, the main problem is that, despite shielding, organs which are not the focus of the treatment get irradiated anyway. This affects the bladder and the bowel in particular. Diarrhoea and nausea are common, but can be made more bearable by using medication. Symptoms like cystitis may occur, but these usually get better.

The vagina and ovaries are also affected. The ovaries will stop working, so you are likely to be given hormone replacement therapy afterwards. The vagina shrinks and becomes less elastic, partly as a direct effect of the radiation, but also because of the loss of the oestrogen hormone from the ovaries. Following radiotherapy, it is important to try to have sex quite soon, or the shrinkage can become permanent. This is another reason why radiotherapy is generally avoided in young women.

CHEMOTHERAPY

As its name suggests, this involves treatment using chemicals, given either by mouth or by injection. They are also called cytotoxics (*cyto* means cell) because they kill cells. Unfortunately, they lack discrimination and tend to kill normal as well as abnormal cells, so they often have unpleasant side effects. These can include nausea, vomiting and hair loss. They are not a first-line treatment for cervical cancer and are used mainly in late-stage cancer. Sometimes they are given before or after surgery or radiotherapy, to try to shrink the tumour. In general they are still being used mostly in research studies, rather than in routine treatment.

HOW SUCCESSFUL ARE THE TREATMENTS?

Specific predictions can be made only by the gynaecologist who is dealing with the case. Do not be afraid to ask. In general terms, if the cancer is caught early enough, before the lymph nodes are involved, there is a good chance of cure, around 80 to 90 per cent. However, if the lymph nodes are already involved and therefore the cancer has managed to spread to other parts of the body, the chance of success is only 50 per cent: this means that half the women with later-stage cancers die within five years. And remember that many of those women will not have noticed anything wrong until it was too late. Once again, let me remind you of the importance of regular screening.

7

Why me?
The possible causes of
CIN and cervical cancer

It has been known for over a century that cervical cancer is closely associated with sexual activity. However, as we shall see, there must be other factors involved.

In 1842 an Italian doctor called Rigoni-Stern noticed that nuns very rarely developed cancer of the cervix. When he looked into this more deeply, he found that not all nuns seemed to be 'immune' – women who had been married before entering the order appeared to be at roughly the same risk as the general population. He concluded that virginity must be the protective factor.

SEXUAL BEHAVIOUR

Rigoni-Stern's work was largely ignored for over a hundred years, until a Canadian doctor repeated the study, looking at nuns in Quebec.

This opened the floodgates for research into this area

in the 1950s. Suddenly everyone was interested in cervical cancer. Within a few years it had been established that the disease was particularly common in women who worked as prostitutes, and that a very important risk factor was the age at which a woman first had sex. Indeed, it has been found that women who start having sex below the age of seventeen have more than twice the risk of those who start after the age of twenty. Also, the more partners a woman had, the greater her risk: women with four partners had twice the risk of those who had only one.

Soon it was found that young age at first pregnancy placed a woman at risk, while women with few or no pregnancies seemed less at risk than those who had many pregnancies. Divorced, widowed or separated women were at risk. It was even claimed that women who attended church regularly were less likely to develop the disease than their non-attending counterparts.

Scientists started to look at the differences in incidence in various countries, and found them to be quite striking. Colombia had an incidence nearly one hundred times greater than that of Israel; the United States and Europe were somewhere in-between. Then they looked at different ethnic groups. It was interesting that Jewish women tended to have the same incidence regardless of which country they lived in. The scientists then compared Jewish women, white American women and non-white Americans who all lived in the same place, New York. Non-white American women had the highest incidence, Jewish women the lowest and white Americans were in-between.

Next, it was noticed that there was a difference between the social classes, and also within each social class. At that time, and often to this day, social-class grading was usually done according to the occupation of the husband. (The author refrains from comment, except to say that in the last few years, details relating to social class have no longer been requested on the cervical smear form.) It was found that there was a much higher incidence of cervical cancer in the lower social classes.

However, regardless of social class, there was a higher incidence among women married to men whose jobs involved travel and long periods away from home, for example sailors, long-distance lorry drivers, soldiers and so on. The table opposite shows you how the risks varied according to the husband's occupation.

So the doctors and scientists looked at all these pieces of information and tried to find something that would link them together. The conclusion seemed inescapable: it must relate to the woman's sexual behaviour. What do prostitutes, widows, divorced women, women who marry very young or start having sex very young, have in common? They are likely to have more than one sexual partner in their lifetime. So started the 'cervical cancer is a disease of promiscuity' story. Nuns have no sexual partners, Jewish women and very religious women of any denomination tend to have only one partner – it all seemed to fit.

Then a few little contradictions started to creep in. How come cervical cancer was very common in upper-social-class women in Colombia, who were usually faithful to their husbands? And who was more likely to have large numbers of sexual partners, the sailor or his wife? In the late 1960s the attention therefore turned to men.

An important study looked at men whose first wives had died of cervical cancer. It was found that their subsequent wives were nearly three times as likely to

Risk of cervical cancer by social class and husband's occupation in married women (England and Wales 1959–63)

Social Class	Occupation of husband	Woman's risk of cervical cancer (higher number equals higher risk)
I	All occupations	34
	Clergymen	12
	Scientists	17
	Civil engineers	60
II	All occupations	64
	Teachers	30
	Senior government officials	40
	Publicans and innkeepers	120
	Lodging house and hotel keepers	150
III	All occupations	100
	Clerks of work	40
	Clerks	64
	Crane and hoist operators	159
	Drivers of road goods vehicles	168
IV	All occupations	116
	Shopkeepers and assistants	71
	Gardeners and groundsmen	98
	Fishermen	257
	Boatmen	263

Risk of cervical cancer defined by husband's occupation

develop the disease. The sexual behaviour of men in Colombia was then studied, and it was found that the well-to-do Colombian man was accustomed to visiting prostitutes on a regular basis, while his wife remained faithful. A further study looked specifically at men, to see how their numbers of partners influenced their wives' risk of cervical cancer (the wives in the study all said they had had only one partner, their husband). If the man had had more than fifteen partners, his wife's risk of developing cervical cancer was nearly eight times greater than if he had only had one partner. All these studies led to the concept of the high-risk male, which will be discussed in greater detail in the next chapter.

So it was not just the sexual behaviour of women which was important – the behaviour of men had to be taken into account as well. On the basis of the new findings, three models of behaviour were drawn up to try to explain the differences in incidence between different countries, ethnic groups and religious denominations (see the table opposite).

In a type-A society, both the woman and the man have only one sexual partner, i.e. each other. This is the type of behaviour found among religious Jews and certain other religious denominations. The incidence of cervical cancer is very low.

In a type-B society, the woman has only one partner, but the man has many. This was the case in Colombia and also in Victorian England. The incidence of cervical cancer is very high.

In a type-C society both the man and the woman have more than one partner, but neither has a large number of partners. This is the general pattern of behaviour in Europe and the United States today. The incidence of cervical cancer is above that of type-A, but

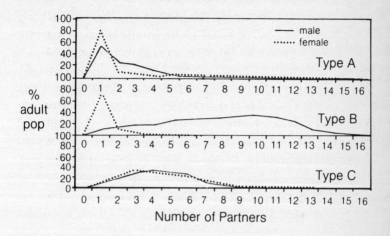

Patterns of behaviour in three types of society

well below that of type-B societies.

OTHER SUSPECTED FACTORS

Having established that cervical cancer was in some way related to sex, the next obvious question was: what is it that passes between a man and a woman to cause the disease? And it did not take long for people to start looking at sperm. It has been shown that sperm can become attached to the very cells on the cervix that can eventually become abnormal. Certain types of protein, which are part of the sperm head, may be able to interfere in some way with the functions of the cell. In addition, sperm may be able to reduce the immune (defensive) response of the cervical cells. The exact mechanisms for these effects are unknown, and they are certainly weak; however, it is possible that the proteins help some other agent to cause abnormalities in the cells. This is known as being a 'cofactor', and we will come across this again later. One study has also shown that the wart virus (which will be discussed in the next chapter) can be passed on through semen.

The next suggestion was that it might be something to do with personal hygiene. This was based mainly on the fact that there was a low incidence amongst Jewish women, whose partners are circumcised. Perhaps smegma, the substance which collects under the foreskin, had something to do with it? The idea of personal hygiene seemed to tie in well with the social-class variation. A man coming home after a long day's work at the coal face might well be more 'dirty' than an office clerk. Unfortunately for this theory, the facts just did not add up. For example, studies were made of a tribe in Malaysia. The men are uncircumcised, the girls marry at about the age of fourteen and they have never heard of the idea of hygiene. In addition the women start having children immediately after their marriage and tend to have a large number (they haven't heard of contraception either). Despite all this, their incidence of cervical cancer is very low. Of more significance is the fact that they do not have premarital sex, and remain faithful to each other after marriage. And, of course, this is also the more likely explanation for the low incidence of cervical cancer among Jews. In this context, it is interesting to note that more recent work suggests that the incidence of cervical cancer in non-orthodox Jewish women is rising: Jewish men are still usually circumcised, whether orthodox or not, but presumably the main difference lies in a less strict code of sexual behaviour.

SMOKING

In recent years, smoking has become a focus of attention. An association between smoking and cervical cancer was noticed as long ago as 1977, but at first it was dismissed as being improbable – after all, how does the smoke get all the way down to the cervix? And maybe it was just that women who smoked were also more likely to have sex young and to have more partners. However, even when those factors were taken into account, smokers still appeared to be at greater risk than non-smokers. The exact degree of the increase in risk varies from study to study, but that of cancer appears to be increased by about a factor of two, and that of CIN 3 (the third stage of abnormal cells) increased by up to twelve times.

Then, in the 1980s, several studies showed that components of cigarette smoke, including nicotine and cotinine, were found in high concentrations in cervical mucus. The amounts were even higher than in the blood of the same women, so it looked as though, for some reason, these potentially cancer-producing substances were congregating around the cervix. Thus, suddenly, there was an obvious way in which smoking could be contributing to the risk of cervical cancer.

There is another way in which smoke-related poisons might be involved: they might reduce the immune (defence) mechanisms of the cervical cells. Studies have shown that the number of special immune cells in the cervix, called Langerhans cells (after a doctor, Paul Langerhans), is reduced in women who have CIN. There are several other types of immune cell which can be similarly affected. It has also been shown that these immune cells are reduced in number in women who smoke. Thus, the same thing happens in both cases. If there are fewer immune cells, the cervical cells are less able to defend themselves against attackers. Thus, smoking may help some other, probably sexually transmitted agent, to cause cervical cancer. Once again, it may be acting as a cofactor.

DIET

In the last ten years there has been some suggestion that a diet deficient in certain vitamins may increase the risk of cervical cancer. However, the picture is still rather unclear, with studies giving conflicting results, both as to whether vitamins are involved at all and as to which vitamins may be important. The ones that may be of interest are vitamin C, vitamin E and beta-carotene, which is part of vitamin A. These vitamins have something in common: they all mop up free radicals, which are nasty substances, thought to be involved in a number of cancers. Thus, the idea that they may be useful is plausible. However, it is possible that only a severe deficiency is important: the studies suggesting a link have tended to be from the Third World, in areas where the diet is very poor.

So far, there is no evidence that taking extra vitamin supplements is of any use, either in prevention or cure, but since no one has any idea of the possible doses needed, studies have not been very satisfactory. It is in any case a minefield in which to try to do research. Measuring people's intake of vitamins is fraught with problems: questionnaires may not give a good representation of a person's diet, may not be filled in properly, or may be misunderstood. Blood tests are quite expensive, difficult to do and in any case not popular. There are so many other things that can affect blood–vitamin levels: for example, it is known that smokers who eat the same amount of vitamins as non-smokers have lower levels of the vitamin in their blood. Presumably, smokers do not absorb their vitamins so well. And we have seen that smoking may in any case increase the risk of cancer.

At present it is impossible to be sure what effect, if any, vitamins may have. Research is continuing, but I doubt whether there will be definite answers for some time.

CONTRACEPTION

Studies looking at contraceptive use and cervical cancer are rather obviously hampered by the fact that the majority of people use contraception when they are having sex. And since sex itself seems to be the most important risk factor, it is difficult to separate the effects of one from the other. In addition, it is possible that people choosing different methods of contraception also behave differently – they may have different numbers of partners, different smoking habits and so on.

However, if the main cause of cervical cancer is a sexually transmitted agent, then barrier methods of contraception are likely to be protective. This does appear to be the case. Use of diaphragms or of condoms is associated with a reduced risk of cervical cancer. Interestingly, the use of spermicides alone (for example, foams) also appears to reduce the risk. Spermicides are designed to kill or immobilise sperm, but can also have some effect on bacteria, possibly even on viruses.

Intrauterine contraceptive devices (IUDs) and pro-gestogen-only pills (POPs) do not appear to have any effect on cervical cancer risk. This is now also considered true of the injectable progestogen, Depo Provera. In the past, some studies suggested a slight increase in risk for users of this method, but they were always hampered by not adjusting for other known risk factors, such as numbers of sexual partners and smoking. (As a group, Depo Provera users are known to be more likely to smoke than users of a number of other contraceptive methods.) In 1992, the results of a large World Health Organisation study were published. This was a long-running study, and from 1984 the researchers had decided to include details of smoking, when the link with cervical cancer became established. In this way they were able to take into account more risk factors than previous studies had done, and they found no increase in risk for users of Depo Provera.

The relationship between the use of the combined oral contraceptive pill and the risk of cervical cancer remains controversial. Here we come across two pitfalls: first, the usual one of other known risk factors confusing the issue, and secondly, the fact that the formulation of the pill has been changing during the last thirty years. Until the mid-1980s, studies looking at pill use and at the risk of cervical cancer did not take smoking history into account. Nowadays, women taking the pill are advised not to smoke, mainly because of the risk of heart disease. However, when the pill was first introduced, the risks of smoking in relation to pill use and heart disease were not appreciated. Indeed, these high-dose pills were being handed out even to women smokers who were over 35 years old, right up to the early 1980s. It was only then that the risks of heart disease became apparent, and it was also around then that the link between smoking and cervical cancer became established.

In the 1960s and 1970s, for a woman to be on the pill was daring and liberated: so was smoking. It is therefore not too surprising that pill users were more likely to smoke than were users of other contraceptive methods. Since smokers have been shown to have more sexual partners than non-smokers, there would be a higher proportion of pill users also in this category. We have already seen that the number of sexual partners is an important risk factor in its own right. I am sure you can already see that all this makes trying to look at pill use on its own very difficult.

The dose of hormones in the pill has come down progressively during the last thirty years. Not only that, but the hormones themselves have been modified. Low-dose pills have been around since the early 1980s, but the newest pills only since the mid to late 1980s. Research studies take many years to conduct and to analyse: how do we know whether the results of studies looking at women using older, high-dose pills are relevant to women today?

As an interesting aside on this point, a study has recently been published of the risks of breast cancer in users of both low- and high-dose pills. Although there was a slight increase in risk for long-term users of high-dose pills, this was not true for users of the low-dose pills: their risk was unaffected by pill use. Unfortunately, we do not yet have data on the risk of cervical cancer in users of low-dose pills, since all the studies so far relate to high-dose pills.

The World Health Organisation study last published results regarding cervical cancer and pill use in 1985. This means that they were not able to adjust for smoking, since they only began to do that in 1984 (see page 124). Also they were looking at users of high-dose pills. The study showed a very small increase in risk overall, but did show that the risk tended to increase with long-term use. Women who had used the pill for more than five years had one and a half times the risk of non-users. The authors themselves stated in the paper that this might be accounted for by not adjusting for smoking and other risk factors.

At present, it is not possible to say whether the association between pill use and cervical cancer is a real one. At worst, though, it would appear that the pill may act as a 'helper' to some other, probably sexually transmitted agent. Even then, its effect would be weaker than that of smoking.

It is also important to remember that the pill is an extremely effective contraceptive, giving a 99 per cent protection against pregnancy. Pregnancy can be a cause of a number of health problems, not only a possible risk factor for cervical cancer.

What, then, should be the advice for a pill user today? Well, the most obvious thing is to have regular smears: this is the single most important action you can take, regardless of your method of contraception. If you are very worried about cervical cancer, a belt and braces approach would be to use a barrier method in addition to the pill: although barriers may protect your cervix, remember they are not as effective as the pill in terms of contraception.

Even if you have an abnormal smear, even if you have to have treatment, you can carry on taking the pill. Remember that there is no definite evidence that the pill is implicated in increasing the risk of cervical cancer: it may yet turn out to have been due to incomplete adjustment for other risk factors. In addition, there is no evidence to suggest that use of the pill makes an abnormal smear get worse, or makes a recurrence more likely.

DEFICIENCIES OF THE IMMUNE SYSTEM

The immune system is the body's defence mechanism against foreign invaders, whether they are infections or cancers. One would therefore expect that if cervical cancer is primarily due to a sexually transmitted agent, women who for some reason have an impaired immune system would be more likely to develop it.

We have already seen that smoking may reduce the number of immune cells in the cervix and that smokers are at greater risk of developing cervical cancer.

Studies have looked at women whose immune systems are depressed for other reasons. For example, women who have kidney transplants have to take strong medication to suppress their immune system: otherwise they will reject their new kidney as a 'foreign invader'. These women have been found to be at increased risk of a number of cancers, including cervical cancer.

Women who are being treated for other cancers using chemotherapy have also been studied. These drugs are potent cell poisons and are known to depress the immune system: once again, such women are at higher risk of developing cervical cancer.

The Human Immunodeficiency Virus (HIV) which causes Acquired Immune Deficiency Syndrome (AIDS) is an obvious cause of reduced immunity, and indeed, HIV-positive women have been shown to be more likely to have CIN. However, a problem with looking at HIV-positive women is that they are likely to have other risk factors for cervical cancer. A recent study is interesting, in which HIV-negative women attending a department of genitourinary medicine were compared with HIV-positive women in the same department. Some of the HIV-positive women were perfectly healthy, while others were beginning to develop AIDS-related illnesses. They found that there was no difference in terms of CIN between the HIV-negative women and the healthy HIV-positive women. However, the HIV-positive women who were showing signs of immune deficiency were more likely to have CIN.

PREGNANCY AND ADOLESCENCE

Women who become pregnant young and who have several pregnancies appear to be more at risk of cervical cancer, though partly this effect is due to having had sex under the age of 20. Nevertheless, pregnancy does seem to be a risk factor in its own right.

Pregnancy is another time when the immune system is relatively suppressed. After all, the growing baby is really a 'foreign body' and needs to be protected from destruction by the immune system. It is not altogether surprising, therefore, that women who have had several pregnancies may be more likely to develop cervical cancer. It used to be thought that CIN also progressed faster during pregnancy, but it may be that the pregnant cervix simply looks worse than it really is.

Pregnancy and adolescence do have something in common. During both, a great deal of activity goes on in the transformation zone. As you will remember from Chapter 2, it is in this area that soft columnar cells change to become tough squamous cells – squamous metaplasia. This is a perfectly normal process, but it is at this time that cells are most vulnerable to any outside influences which might cause them to develop in an abnormal way. During both pregnancy and adolescence, squamous metaplasia goes on at a much faster rate and involves a larger number of cells. This means there are more cells around that are vulnerable to attack.

VIRUSES

In the 1960s scientists everywhere were searching for a sexually transmitted 'agent' which could be the cause of cervical cancer. The idea of viruses being a cause of cancer was one that had long been popular, so it was not surprising that attention soon turned to them. The next chapter deals with this, perhaps most significant, part of the story.

8

The role of viruses

WHAT IS A VIRUS?

Louis Pasteur and his pupil, Emile Roux, were the first scientists to show that something even smaller than bacteria could cause disease in both animals and man. Their work on the rabies virus in the 1880s paved the way for years of intensive research into viruses. The microscopes used at that time were not powerful enough to show up any kind of virus, so these micro-organisms were, in effect, invisible. Scientists could only guess at what they might be like.

There was only one way to study the effects of a virus; a solution made from diseased tissue was passed through a very fine filter, with holes so small that no ordinary cells or bacteria could get through. This filtered solution was then injected into an animal; the animal still developed the disease, showing that a disease-causing agent had remained in the solution after it was filtered.

This was a big step forward, but they still did not know how the solutions caused disease. The major breakthrough did not come until 1935, when an American scientist, Wendell Stanley, managed to form crystals from a solution. When he redissolved the crystals in water, they still caused disease. This made it look as though viruses were not alive at all, but just complicated proteins.

The next advance was the discovery that viruses contained either RNA (ribonucleic acid) or DNA (deoxyribonucleic acid). These substances are found in the nucleus of a cell. They are the building blocks of genes, which can be inherited and are the code for different types of cell.

A virus uses its own DNA or RNA to take control of the cell, rather like a terrorist hijacking an aeroplane. It will override the cell's own DNA or RNA and thus use the cell to reproduce itself. However, some viruses may simply enter the cell and lie dormant for long periods of time; this is true of the human papillomavirus, which I shall be discussing in detail later. Viruses cannot function without a host cell to provide for their needs; in this they are different from bacteria, which are self-sufficient.

THE IMMUNE RESPONSE

Viruses are foreign invaders and the body responds by producing an army. White blood cells immediately start manufacturing special proteins designed to fight a particular virus type. This is rather like having an inbuilt system that can work out what is in a poison and then produce the antidote. These special proteins are called antibodies and they travel in the bloodstream to wherever they are needed. This forms the basis of immunity.

Once the body has produced a particular antibody, it retains the 'blueprint' for future reference. Thus, if the same virus tries to invade again, the correct antibody

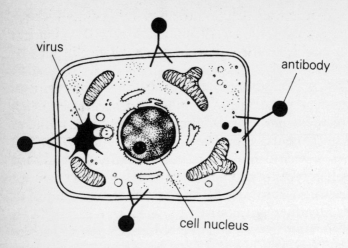

virus

antibody

cell nucleus

The immune response involves antibodies which latch on to a cell after a virus has invaded it

can be produced much more quickly. The body's defence is therefore stronger and the virus has less chance of winning.

Each virus triggers the manufacture of an antibody type that is specific to itself. This means the body has to produce a new variety of antibody every time a new type of virus comes along. You will almost certainly have noticed that having flu once does not protect you from getting it again: the next attack is by a different kind of flu virus and so you have no instant army waiting to protect you against it. However, if you have had, say, chicken pox, you are very unlikely to get it again because the body will recognise the virus – since it will be the same kind – when you come in contact with it once more.

Vaccines are based on this principle. A vaccine is designed to stimulate the body to produce antibodies against a particular virus or bacterium, so that it will have a ready army when the real thing comes along. The vaccine itself is very similar to the virus, but has been made harmless, like a cobra which has had its fangs removed.

Once a blueprint has been created, small numbers of the specific antibodies circulate in the blood even when there is no infection. This is the way in which your immunity can be checked: for example, a blood test can prove whether you are immune to German measles (Rubella), by seeing whether you already have the correct antibodies. This is an important concept, which I shall mention again later.

VIRUSES AND CANCER

At first, scientists looked only to see if viruses caused infectious diseases, like bacteria do, but in 1911 another French scientist, Rous, demonstrated that a filtered solution could produce cancer in birds. This was the beginning of what became a rapidly expanding area of research. Indeed, people began to think that viruses were the cause of *all* cancers.

Numerous examples of viral cancers started to be found in animals. A virus was found to cause leukaemia in cats, another to cause skin cancer in rabbits, yet another to cause breast cancer in mice. The list is long and continues to grow. Human cancers increasingly became associated with viruses. For example, the virus which causes a type of glandular fever may occasionally also cause cancer of the nasal passages and a type of lymphoma (cancer of the lymph nodes). Another example is provided by one of the viruses that causes hepatitis and can also cause liver cancer.

It seemed obvious, therefore, to search for a viral cause of cervical cancer. In fact, viruses of several kinds

are not too difficult to find in cervical cancer or in CIN
(cervical intra-epithelial neoplasia, or abnormal cells,
see Chapter 2); the problem is to show that they are not
just 'innocent bystanders'. This is an important distinction. To use an analogy: just because someone happens
to be found at the scene of a crime does not automati-
cally mean he is guilty of murder.

There have been three main contenders for the role
of the 'cervical cancer virus'. These are the cytomegalovirus, herpes simplex virus and human papillomavirus.

Cytomegalovirus

This is a very common virus. It may cause a flu-like
illness or even, occasionally, a type of glandular fever,
but most people are quite unaware that they have had
the infection. If caught during pregnancy it can be
dangerous, because it can affect the baby (rather like
German measles).

Cytomegalovirus (CMV) can also be sexually transmitted and has been found in tissue from the cervix, as
well as in semen. This fact led to suspicion that it might
be a cause of cervical cancer. Indeed, it was found to be
present more often in cervical cancer than in normal
tissue. However, it is so common that it is difficult to
explain why more women have not developed cancer.
It is also quite possible that, once cells have become
weakened by the real cancer agent, CMV makes the
most of an easy opportunity to invade. It seems
unlikely that CMV will prove to be important in the
causation of cervical cancer.

Herpes Simplex Virus

This virus has had a troubled career. In the late 1960s, herpes (HSV) shot to prominence and enjoyed nearly a decade of being 'the' virus. In the 1980s it was denounced as a fraud and sank into obscurity. However, in the last few years it has made a modest comeback, with renewed interest in its possible role.

There are two kinds of herpes virus, HSV 1, which usually causes cold sores, and HSV 2, which usually causes genital herpes (just to complicate matters, they can occasionally swap over). Most interest has centred around HSV 2.

The herpes virus was already known to be capable of causing kidney tumours in frogs. In addition, it is a close relative of the glandular fever virus (the Epstein Barr virus), which is associated with two types of cancer in humans. Around 1966 it was noticed that women who suffered from genital herpes seemed to have more than their fair share of abnormal smears. Scientists therefore started looking for antibodies to HSV 2 in women with cervical cancer (antibodies have been explained in detail earlier in this chapter. If a person has antibodies to a virus in their blood, it means that at some point they have been infected with that virus. It is like a fingerprint left behind long after the culprit has gone). The scientists found that a high proportion of women with cervical cancer had these antibodies, while a group of women who were similar, but did not have cervical cancer, were much less likely to have such antibodies. This looked very promising.

Unfortunately, later studies did not always agree. The proportion of women with cervical cancer who had antibodies to HSV 2 could vary from as high as 90 per cent to as low as 30 per cent. Herpes is a highly infectious disease, and it was quite possible that these figures simply reflected the level of infection in a given area. The studies were, after all, being done during the 'swinging sixties' and early 1970s, when liberated behaviour resulted in an increase in all forms of sexually transmitted disease.

In the 1970s, researchers started to look at the activity of viruses after they had got inside the cells. As I mentioned earlier, viruses are made up of genetic material, in the form of DNA or RNA; some viruses incorporate their own DNA into that of the cell and in this way the cell's 'instructions' are changed and the virus takes control. However, when scientists looked at cells which had been attacked by the herpes virus, they found that very little, if any, of this incorporation had taken place. The virus seemed to have damaged the cells in various ways, but did not appear to have taken control. It seemed that the herpes virus was behaving in a 'hit and run' fashion. This made it much less likely that the herpes virus could be an important cause of cervical cancer on its own. However, by damaging the cells, it might make them more vulnerable to any further attack, so it might act as a primer for a more important agent.

This role has become of more interest in the last few years. A study has looked at the risk of cervical cancer in women who had HSV 2, human papillomavirus (see below), or both together. The women who had only HSV 2 showed very little increase in their risk of cervical cancer, while those who had only human papillomavirus did have an increased risk. However, there was a quite dramatic effect in the women who had both types of virus: these women were twice as likely to have cervical cancer as those who had the human papillomavirus on its own. This suggests that the two viruses interact, with the herpes virus helping the human papillomavirus in some way. I shall be discussing this again later.

Having mentioned it, let us now look at the human papillomavirus, which has taken over as 'the virus of the moment'. When scientists began to be disillusioned with the herpes theory, they started to notice that the wart virus, or human papillomavirus (HPV), was often found in cervical cancer tissue. Could this be the virus they had been looking for?

THE HUMAN PAPILLOMAVIRUS (HPV OR WART VIRUS)

It had been known since 1907 that skin warts could be transmitted by a cell-free solution, that is, by some sort of submicroscopic infective agent. Then, in 1933, it was shown that a wart virus caused skin cancer in cottontail rabbits. However, an interesting feature emerged: the wart virus did not always cause cancer; it seemed to need help from some other source. For example, a wart virus causes gut cancer in cows, but only if they also eat bracken. Sheep infected with wart virus can get skin cancer, but only in parts of the body directly exposed to sunlight.

In the late 1970s, workers started to look at cells infected with the wart virus. They found not just one wart virus, but many different types, which could be identified by the type of DNA they contained. Although they were all related, they seemed to behave quite differently from each other. For example, the type which causes plantar warts (the common verrucca), shows little interest in infecting cervical cells. In addition, while some types of wart virus could be found in cervical cells, not all of them were incorporated into the cells' DNA, so were probably just innocent bystanders.

As research technology became more sophisticated, it was possible to work out the exact types of wart virus present in different places. Currently there are around sixty-five different types of wart virus and the number identified is growing all the time. Type 1 is the verrucca virus. The genital warts which you can see on the vulva or the penis are usually caused by HPV types 6 or 11. These are often also found in cervical cells, but they are not incorporated into the cells' DNA. However, when types 16, 18, 31, 33 or 35 are found in cervical cells, they *are* usually incorporated into the DNA, and these are the types most often found in cervical cancer.

So it looks as though there are low-risk (that is, unrelated to cancer) wart viruses (types 6 and 11), and high-risk ones (types 16, 18, 31, 33, 35). The trouble is that both low-risk and high-risk types can cause cell changes. It is not possible to tell which is which from a cervical smear or even a biopsy, unless special techniques are used to look at the DNA in the cells. At present the process is expensive and time-consuming, so it is done only in the few hospitals interested in the research.

When a cell is invaded by HPV, characteristic changes can be seen under the microscope. These changes are not part of the 'abnormal cell' spectrum, and the cells that show signs of HPV infection are called koilocytes. You may see this term used on smear reports, though there is now a category in section 23 for 'wart virus' (see the illustration opposite).

Wart virus changes can, however, look similar to abnormal cell changes. In addition, the two can simply occur together. It is not uncommon to see a report of 'borderline dyskaryosis' and 'wart virus change' (see the illustration opposite bottom).

Wart virus changes may have a characteristic appearance on colposcopy and may show up in biopsies. The

22 Cytological pattern		23 Specific infection		24 Management suggested	
inadequate specimen	1	trichomonas	1		
negative	(2)	candida	2	normal recall	1
borderline changes	8	wart virus	(3)	repeat smear in ___ months	2
mild dyskaryosis	3	herpes	4	or after treatment	3
moderate dyskaryosis	7	actinomyces	5	gynaecological referral	4
severe dyskaryosis	4	other (specify)	6	cancel recall	5
severe dyskaryosis/ ? invasive carcinoma	5	**Signature**		**date**	
? glandular neoplasia	6				

Sections 22 and 23 of smear form with 'wart virus' ringed

herpes virus can also cause changes in the cells, which
may be noted in section 23 of the form.

In addition to changes that can be seen in cells,
antibodies are formed to the specific type of wart virus
or viruses that have caused the infection and these
antibodies may be detected in blood samples. Studies
looking at specific types of HPV have shown that
women with cervical cancer are more likely to have

22 Cytological pattern		23 Specific infection		24 Management suggested	
inadequate specimen	1	trichomonas	1		
negative	2	candida	2	normal recall	1
borderline changes	(8)	wart virus	(3)	repeat smear in ___ months	2
mild dyskaryosis	3	herpes	4	or after treatment	3
moderate dyskaryosis	7	actinomyces	5	gynaecological referral	4
severe dyskaryosis	4	other (specify)	6	cancel recall	5
severe dyskaryosis/ ? invasive carcinoma	5	**Signature**		**date**	
? glandular neoplasia	6				

*Sections 22 and 23 of smear form – 'borderline changes'
ringed in 22 and 'wart virus' in 23*

antibodies to, for example, HPV type 16, than well women. However, antibody studies are complicated by the large number of HPV types, and the techniques are still being refined.

In recent years it has been shown that the high-risk types of HPV contain special proteins (called E6 and E7) which are able to 'switch on' the transformation process in cells. I have already referred to the important thing about HPV, which is its ability to incorporate itself into the cell's DNA and use it for its own purposes. It seems that these E6 and E7 proteins can make a cell 'decide' to grow abnormally. This is rather like a science fiction story in which the enemy alien enters someone's brain and makes that person behave in a way that benefits the alien, perhaps killing comrades, taking over the spaceship, and so on.

Evidence for the involvement of HPV types in CIN is increasing all the time. A new technique, called polymerase chain reaction or PCR, has enabled HPV types to be studied in great detail. PCR works rather like an enormous magnifying glass. Only a very tiny amount of the wart virus DNA has to be present. The reagents are primed to recognise a specific variety of DNA. Once it is found, even in only one cell, it will be 'amplified': the reagents will take that piece of DNA, use it as a template and produce a huge number of copies. When enough copies are present, they become identifiable by special techniques and it is then possible to say that a particular virus type is there.

Older techniques were less sensitive, and large amounts of the virus were needed before its presence could be detected. The methods used were also slow and laborious. PCR is relatively quick and simple, and extremely sensitive, being able to detect minute amounts of virus.

This very sensitivity has caused a lot of problems. If you can pick up virus from just one cell, then if a few cells happen to be lying around on the workbench, and are wiped on to your test tube, your next experiment will be rubbish because of contamination. When the method was first being used, embarrassing mistakes were made: scientists began to claim that they could find HPV in 100 per cent of the population. For several years, the whole wart virus story took a nosedive because it appeared that, like herpes or CMV, there was just too much wart virus around for plausibility. Gradually, however, the problem of contamination was recognised, and apologies started to appear in scientific journals.

When studies were done very carefully, it was found that, while HPV was present in the vast majority (around 95 per cent) of women with cervical cancer and CIN, it could be found in less than 20 per cent of women with a normal cervix.

Extremely high sensitivity causes other problems. What does it mean if just one or two cells out of millions are infected with HPV? Does it matter? Indeed, when scientists have simply looked for the presence, in any quantity, of virus, they have found that it is present in anyone who has any kind of cervical cell abnormality. Although this is of some use, it does not tell us what we really want to know: which women have abnormalities that *matter*? After all, if a woman has CIN 1 and it is never going to progress to anything worse, why get her and her doctors worried for no reason?

A couple of recent studies have taken the technique of PCR a stage further. They looked not just for the presence of high-risk wart viruses, but for how much of the virus was there. This is a refinement of the basic PCR method, to actually try to quantify the levels of viral infection. They were particularly interested in type 16, which has the strongest link with cancer. When type 16 was present in great quantity, there was a high chance (90 per cent) that the woman would turn out to have CIN 3, even though her smear showed only a mild abnormality.

In Chapter 2 I discussed the problem of taking a mildly abnormal smear at its word: about a third of such women will turn out to have CIN 2 or 3 already. If these women can be filtered out using the PCR test for HPV, we will know who needs a colposcopy now and who can safely be left a while.

Another study has looked at the use of the HPV PCR test in cervical screening. Women who were having routine smears had the new test as well. Fortunately the same spatula/brush sample can be used for both the HPV PCR and the smear, it is just processed in two different ways. Any woman who had either an abnormal smear or a high level of HPV (the types being looked at were 16, 18, 31 and 33) had a colposcopy.

The study found that twice as much high grade CIN (2 and 3) was picked up by the HPV test as by the cervical smear. The majority of abnormalities were in fact detected using just HPV types 16 and 31, though the other two also made a significant contribution. Worryingly, nearly a third of the CIN 3 abnormalities were missed by the smear. However, it must be said that there were a small number of abnormalities which were picked up by the smear and missed by the HPV test: maybe there are other important HPV types which were not included in this study. Perhaps to achieve the best results we will need to use a combination of HPV testing and cervical smears.

When you take all these studies together, the evidence that high-risk HPV types are the main cause of cervical cancer is very strong. You may be asking, 'Why haven't we started using the PCR test already, if it is so good?', and even, 'Why don't we just abandon the smear, the PCR test is better?' The answer is that bigger studies are needed first. Remember that at the start, research studies are always small, because no one is going to throw lots of money and time at something that may not work. Similarly, you would not want to abandon a tried and tested (even if imperfect) method for one which has shown promise but might yet turn out to be a false hope. So the next few years are likely to be very exciting, as larger studies begin to be carried out. If you are keen to have the test, ask around to see if any doctors in your area are involved in a study; you may find you are eligible to join.

So much wart virus floating around: but where does it all come from? To answer that question, several studies have been done of men. One looked at a group of men whose partners had CIN. Over two-thirds of the men were found to have wart virus infections of the penis. Not all of them had visible warts, however; nearly half had infections which showed up only when acetic acid was used, just as in colposcopy (see page 64). (Areas of the penis which have wart virus infection show up with acetic acid and have a characteristic appearance.)

Now, of course, it could be argued that the men got their infection from their female partners. However, studies have gone on to show that women who previously had normal smears and showed no signs of wart virus infection are more likely to develop both visible genital warts and CIN if they have a long-term faithful relationship with a man who has warts. A similar study, looking at virgins who became the partners of men with genital warts also showed that the women were much more likely (in fact, almost certain) to develop warts themselves.

This fits in well with the concept of the high-risk male, which was first mentioned in Chapter 7. Men may, in fact, be unaware they have a high-risk wart virus infection. The problem, as I mentioned earlier, is that the types which cause visible warts (6 and 11) are not the important ones as far as cervical cancer is concerned. It is the invisible ones, for example, HPV types 16, 18, 31, 33 and 35, which are to blame. Men who have visible warts may have other areas of wart virus infection with, say, type 16, of which they, their partners and their doctors are quite unaware. These areas will show up only if they are painted with acetic acid. Similarly, men who have no visible warts at all may still have wart virus infection. Unfortunately, treatment is available only for visible warts, as it is impractical (and painful) to try to treat large areas of essentially normal skin.

Why isn't there an epidemic of penile cancer if so many men are infected? The answer lies in the difference between the cells on the cervix and the penis. In Chapter 2 I mentioned that the vulnerable area on the cervix is the transformation zone, where soft columnar cells change into hard, squamous cells. Cells which are in the process of change can be easily attacked by the wart virus. However, no such change occurs in the cells of the penis. The cells there are all tough squamous cells and are very resistant to attack. Penile cancer is very rare indeed.

Another question you may ask is, 'Why don't all women with wart virus develop cervical cancer?' Part of the answer is that not all types of wart virus are dangerous, as I have mentioned before. However, just to confuse matters, it seems that not even all the women who have high-risk HPV types develop cancer. In addition, in some people both warts and CIN disappear without any treatment. What makes them so special?

You may remember that, earlier in this chapter, I mentioned that whenever wart viruses cause cancer, they seem to need help from some other source. An interesting observation has been that people whose immune system is not functioning well seem to be particularly prone to wart virus. I have already mentioned that women, such as cancer or kidney-transplant patients, who are on drugs to suppress their immune response, have been shown to be more likely to develop CIN and cervical cancer (see Chapter 7). Such women are also much more likely to develop warts. The same thing applies to women who are pregnant and also to women who are HIV positive, or have AIDS (also mentioned in the previous chapter).

Thus it would appear that anything which weakens the body's immune system makes it easier for wart viruses to invade. This also applies to smoking, which, as we saw in the previous chapter, is now recognised as a risk factor for cervical cancer. Indeed, men who smoke have been shown to be more likely to have wart virus infection of the penis. Interestingly, smoking has also emerged as a risk factor for penile cancer, though there is still little evidence of any relationship between penile and cervical cancers.

Earlier in this chapter, I mentioned a study looking at the interaction between HPV and the herpes virus: it would appear that the herpes virus may be acting as another type of helper, or cofactor, to allow HPV to invade more easily.

Smoking and herpes are only two possible sources of help for the wart virus; there may be many others.

Sperm proteins, mentioned in Chapter 7, may also act in this way. The necessity for cofactors may well turn out to be the reason why one woman has HPV infection and develops cancer, while another woman can have the same type of HPV but stays well. A great deal of research is still needed in this area.

CAN I PREVENT MYSELF CATCHING THE WART VIRUS?

As with any sexually transmitted disease, condoms will offer protection; the diaphragm is likely to be less effective, since the vagina and cervix will still come in contact with the virus. It would also seem sensible to avoid smoking. The big problem, of course, is that you can't tell a man has the wart virus just by looking.

Any woman who has had warts or herpes herself, or is the partner of a man who has either of these infections, should have regular smears. That way, if any abnormal cell changes do occur, they will be discovered early and treated before they become serious. Although, as we have seen, the HPV types causing visible warts are not dangerous, at present you cannot tell if you also have the high-risk types from a smear or by looking. Should the smears looking for abnormal cell changes be taken more frequently than every three years? Perhaps, if you knew you had one of the high-risk HPV types. However, the chances are that you don't know and also that there is no way you can find out at present. Having frequent smears if you have low-risk HPV types is not likely to be helpful and may just make you more anxious. Opinions are still divided as to the best way to deal with this problem: if HPV DNA testing became widely available, it might provide the answer (see also Chapter 11).

Both men and women who develop visible genital

warts are often very upset at the inference that they must have been unfaithful, especially since they are often in a long-term monogamous relationship. However, the incubation period of the virus can be very long, even years. So a virus you caught in a previous relationship may suddenly and embarrassingly surface much later.

TREATMENT OF WART VIRUS INFECTIONS

If viruses are a risk factor for cervical cancer, is there any way of getting rid of them before abnormal cell changes occur? And will the virus still be there after treatment for CIN? If only we had definite answers to these questions.

Viruses are in fact very difficult to 'kill', since they are only susceptible when they are reproducing. Often the only way to eliminate them is to kill the cells which are supporting them. If they have invaded a large number of cells, there is a danger that treatment aimed at eliminating the virus may kill the person as well.

So far, no treatment has been found which eradicates viruses completely and permanently. For example, a medicine called acyclovir is useful in the treatment of a herpes attack. It stops the replication of the herpes virus in infected cells, but leaves normal uninfected cells untouched. It therefore has very few side effects. Unfortunately, because it affects only cells in which the virus is replicating, it has no effect on cells where the virus is lying dormant, so in time these will surface and cause another attack.

Local treatments for visible warts all suffer the disadvantage that, obviously, they will work only where they are applied. As we have seen, HPV may be present in cells without causing visible warts; indeed, the more dangerous types (those associated with cancer) are precisely the ones that are 'invisible'. This does not mean, however, that visible warts should be ignored. They can become very large and unsightly. The visible warts also act as a warning of possible risk to the cervix; a third of women who have visible genital warts also have CIN. The high-risk wart viruses seem to travel alongside the low-risk ones, so it is common to be infected with both types at the same time.

There are several local treatments for warts. The ones most commonly used are paints, based on a compound called podophyllum, available as podophyllin paint or podophyllotoxin (Condyline, Warticon). Treatment can be time-consuming as the paint has to be applied regularly, often for several weeks, before the warts disappear. The podophyllotoxin preparations have the advantage of being usable by the patient at home (though they still have to be prescribed); however, the disadvantage is that many people then overdo the treatment in an effort to cure themselves more quickly, and end up with pain, irritation and even burns. If you use these treatments, it really is best to follow the instructions.

An acid, called trichloracetic acid, is also used, but only very carefully, as it can easily cause burns. The treatments for abnormal cells (such as laser and cryotherapy, see Chapter 5) can be used to treat warts, but again, they are unlikely to eradicate the virus. It is difficult to say which treatment is best; one of the major problems in any study is that warts often go away on their own, only to return later, and it can be difficult to tell whether it was the treatment that made them go away.

Some new treatments are being tried. One of these is based on a very strong drug called 5 fluorouracil. It is given by injection in cancer chemotherapy, but has also been made into a cream, which can be used in the treatment of warts and also of wart-infected areas seen on colposcopy. It is so strong that it has to be used with great care to avoid causing severe skin irritation.

A second cancer chemotherapy drug is also being tried. It is called bleomycin and is injected, in very small doses, into warts. It seems to be quite successful in eliminating warts that have resisted all other forms of treatment, but is very tedious, since each wart has to be injected individually.

Since the immune system seems to be important in keeping the virus at bay, ways of boosting the immune response have been studied. Interferon is a substance which the body produces naturally as part of its defence against viruses, and therefore, theoretically at least, if you are given more of it, your immune response should improve. Unfortunately, interferon is also largely responsible for the way we feel when we have a viral infection: tired, shaky, aching joints, generally flu-ish. So when it is injected, that is how the person feels: awful. The side effects have limited its use, especially since it does not really appear to make much difference. Injecting individual warts with interferon has also been tried, again with limited success. Although this approach may have some potential, it is not very useful at present.

Many wart treatments have looked promising, but have turned out to have too many side effects, or just not to work well enough.

You may ask, what is the point of treating women for CIN if they are going to return to an HPV-infected man? Won't they just get it back again? Interestingly, this does not often seem to be the case. It appears that when you remove the vulnerable area, the transforma-tion zone, the risk of developing CIN again is actually quite small, around 10 per cent. Thus, although these women may well still have HPV, and may be in a relationship with a man who has HPV, the virus cannot find vulnerable cells to invade and transform.

There is still a long way to go before we can be really sure of what causes CIN and cervical cancer. However, there is a strong association with certain HPV types and this avenue looks the most promising to date. It is fairly certain that there is no one cause, but several, acting together. Treatment offers a good chance (90 per cent), but not a certain cure. Meanwhile, prevention cannot be guaranteed until we know more about the causes and can treat both the male and female partners effectively.

The only thing that can be done in the interim is to screen women as thoroughly as possible. If we cannot guarantee protection against CIN, at least we should be able to prevent the progression to cancer. The next chapter discusses how this can be done and why it is not always happening at present.

9

The cervical screening controversy: how often should you have a smear?

The first question is: why bother to have smears at all? It's not as stupid as it sounds. Screening is only worthwhile if certain things are true about the disease you are looking for. It must be reasonably common, or a lot of people will go through the bother of having the test when there is virtually no chance of them having the condition. The test should be simple and accurate: people should not be frightened unnecessarily, nor be given false reassurance. The disease you are looking for must be curable; there is no point finding it just to tell people they are going to die. Ideally, the test should be able to detect the disease so early that complete cure is possible in every case.

Cervical cancer is unusual among cancers in that it has a 'warning' stage, CIN, which is present for several years before cancer develops. This makes it a perfect candidate for screening as, theoretically, we should be able to pick up most abnormalities before they have turned into cancer.

'Why should I go for a test? I feel perfectly OK.'

'I heard Edwina Currie say that if you don't screw around you won't get cervical cancer. Well, I've been faithful to my husband all these years, so I don't need a test.'

'Isn't it something you only get if you sleep around? I don't want my neighbours seeing me at the doctor's – they might get the wrong idea.'

Currently, in the UK, around 4000 women a year develop cervical cancer. Many of those women have never had a smear. They do not go for tests for a variety of reasons. Some feel that they will be thought promiscuous because they have heard that the disease is related to promiscuity. Older people are less used to the concept of screening; they only go to see the doctor when they are ill. Many women think the smear is a test for cancer itself, rather than for early-warning changes – and they would rather not know if they have cancer. All these misunderstandings arise from a lack of information about what the smear is, what the possible causes of cervical cancer are, how CIN can be treated and how effective the treatment is. Ignorance breeds fear and women who are frightened of having a smear are very unlikely to go for one. Unfortunately, such women are also unlikely to read a book like this. Maybe you have a friend who has never had a smear and is frightened of having one; please pass on what you have learned to her.

About 80 per cent of the women who develop

cervical cancer are over 40. However, concern has been growing about women under 40. In the early 1960s, only 2 per cent of cervical cancer occurred in young women, but by the mid-1980s the proportion had increased to around 20 per cent. This is illustrated by the graph below, which uses information collected by the Office of Population Censuses and Surveys (OPCS).

Young women have been the group in whom cervical cancer rates have been increasing most rapidly. It is often said that too many smears are taken from young women, who are supposedly at low risk. And yet this large increase in women under 35 has occurred despite the fact that they are having 'too many' smears. One

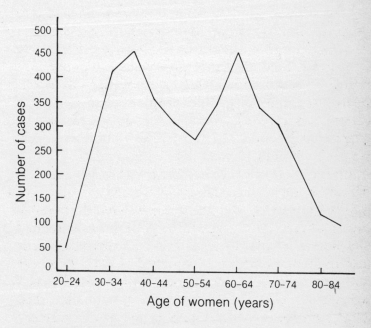

Number of cases of cervical cancer at different ages in 1985 (OPCS 1990) (from P. Soutter: A Practical Guide to Colposcopy, *OUP, 1993)*

can only speculate as to what the figures for cancer would have been if fewer women had had smears.

You will notice from the graph on page 153 that women aged between 45 and 55 seem to be at lower risk. This is also illustrated in the graph below, which shows death rates from cervical cancer at different ages. You will notice that while the rates in women under 45 have generally been going up, those in women over 45 have mainly been coming down. Why should there be such a difference?

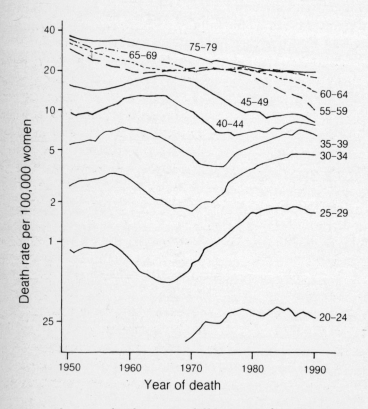

Cervical cancer death rates at different ages between 1950 and 1990 (courtesy Peter Sasieni, Lancet, *338: 818–19)*

In fact, screening is not the reason – after all, why should just one group of women of a certain age benefit more than other groups? The main explanation lies in what is called the cohort effect.

Women who were about 60 in the mid-1970s were born around the time of the First World War and were therefore in their twenties during the Second World War. The war was a time of great uncertainty, husbands and wives were parted for long periods, never knowing if they would see each other again. Soldiers arrived and were posted in small communities, then moved on. I believe the Americans were described as being 'over-sexed and over here'. All this, together with the feeling that the world might end tomorrow, resulted in more relaxed rules of sexual behaviour. This applied to both men and women, of course – while a wife or girlfriend was having an affair with a billeted soldier, who knows what her partner was up to abroad? As a result, these women as a group (or cohort) are at high risk of developing cervical cancer.

However, the group of women who were 40 to 50 years old in the mid-1970s were born just before or during the Second World War and reached their 'dating' years in the mid-1950s. This was a time of strict parental control and moral attitudes, so neither they nor their partners were likely to become sexually active very early, or to have multiple partners. As a result, despite being at a high-risk age, these women are a relatively low-risk group. This is the explanation for the decrease in incidence shown on the graph.

Women who grew up in the climate of the 'swinging sixties' and seventies are a high-risk group. Liberal attitudes were unfortunately accompanied by liberal amounts of sexually transmitted diseases of all kinds. If you were to look at a graph of the incidence of genital herpes and warts, it would show an increase just like that of cervical cancer. Even if the pendulum swings right back because of fear of AIDS, these women will carry a high risk for the rest of their lives.

But there is some good news. You will notice that in the last couple of years covered by the graph on page 154, the curve has levelled off. The incidence of cancer is no longer increasing in younger women (or in any age group). Maybe screening has been having an effect. Perhaps all the publicity about AIDS has also modified people's sexual behaviour. Maybe both have happened together.

Although the incidence in young women seems to have stopped rising, young women should still have regular smears. In addition, educating women while they are young and likely to be receptive to information is the best way to ensure that they continue to have smears as they get older.

HOW OFTEN SHOULD I HAVE A SMEAR?

It's quite simple, actually – the more frequently you have them the better your protection will be.

Yes, it really is that simple. These calculations have been done many times and the answer is always the same. So why is there so much argument about the frequency of smears? You guessed it – money.

There is another aspect, of course. How often would you like to go for a smear? Every five years? Every three years? Every year? Perhaps you're really worried and you'd like to go every six months – why stop at that, get to know your doctor really well, go every week ... you can see that this could become quite ridiculous. I have yet to meet a woman who actually enjoys having a smear (no letters please!). There has to be a point at which you get no extra protection for your discomfort. Also, as mentioned in Chapter 2, some women will be made more anxious, perhaps unnecessarily so, by a mildly abnormal smear. Some may receive treatment they did not really need. The likelihood of all this increases with the frequency at which you have smears.

The figures in the table below are taken from several large international studies, whose results were pooled and published in 1986. Many different studies have been done and the exact numbers vary, but the principle remains the same. The woman who has never been screened is assumed to be the standard, with a risk of 1.0. The woman who has yearly smears is twelve times less likely to develop cancer. However, the woman who has five-yearly smears is only three times less likely to develop cancer. It follows therefore that yearly screening is more effective at protecting against cervical cancer than is five-yearly screening. Put another way, annual smears could possibly prevent 92 per cent of cervical cancer, whereas five-yearly screening could prevent 67 per cent.

There is a contradiction here: if cervical cancer takes around ten years to develop, surely five-yearly

Months since last negative smear	Relative protection
0–11	15.3
12–23	11.9
24–35	8.0
36–47	5.3
48–59	2.8
Never screened	1.0

IARC 1986, BMJ 293: 659–664

screening would be enough? And yet the figures show clearly that it isn't. The problem lies with the smear test itself; smears can be wrong, and give false reassurance. In fact, for the lower grades of CIN, the false negative rate (by which I mean that an abnormality was present, but the smear missed it), can be as high as 50 per cent. Before you go into a panic, let me stress that this does not mean that half the smears taken give the wrong result. What it does mean is that the smear may be missing up to half the cases of mild abnormality. Only about five to ten per cent of women who have smears have a mild abnormality, so only another five to ten per cent will get a false negative result.

Why do smears give the wrong result? There seem to be three reasons. First, the smear may not be taken in the right way or from the right place. In the last few years there have been several scandals where doctors or nurses have been found to be using tongue depressors, for example, to take smears. In another case, a speculum was not being used, so the cervix was not seen. Obviously, whatever instrument is being used, if it is not wiped across the cervix, the result will have no meaning. Similarly, even when the cervix can be seen, part of it may be missed when taking the smear: that might be just the area that was abnormal. In Chapters 1 and 3 I discussed the use of newer instruments which have been designed to try to make smears more accurate. In Chapter 3, I also mentioned the debate about the importance, or otherwise, of endocervical cells. These issues have still not been resolved. Some studies suggest that endocervical cells are important, others say they are not. The bottom line is probably that the person taking the smear is more important than the instrument being used: if you have someone who is good at taking smears, they will probably take a good smear with any (reasonable) instrument you give them. One of the problems with such studies is that the doctors and nurses who volunteer to take part may be precisely the interested and experienced ones who do well anyway. This will not make it easier to tell whether one instrument would be better than another in less experienced hands.

When you go for a smear, you can make a difference to the outcome. If you are tense, it can be very difficult to see your cervix, so try to relax (see the methods suggested on page 176). The doctor or nurse may do their best, but in the end it is you who suffers if the smear was not taken well.

Mistakes can occur in the cytology laboratory. Spare a thought for rows of cytology screeners, who have to look down microscopes all day every day. The vast majority of slides they see – around 90 per cent – will be normal, so their work is unbelievably monotonous. Is it any wonder their concentration can lapse occasionally? Indeed, it has been shown that slides looked at on Monday morning or Friday afternoon are more likely to be misinterpreted. For this reason many laboratories are now performing a quick second check on all smears.

Some smears (around 8 per cent) may be called negative when they are actually not good enough for interpretation, perhaps because there is too much blood obscuring the cells. These may be picked up by a second check.

There is another worrying aspect of the misinterpretation of slides. It has been shown that if two different cytologists look at the same slide, they are quite likely to grade it differently. Not only that, but the same cytologist may give a different opinion on the same slide on different days. The majority of such differences occur in the 'grey areas', rather than the severely abnormal smears. Nevertheless, the consequences can be serious if a woman whose smear shows an abnormality is given the all-clear and advised to have her next smear in five years. It would obviously be better all round if the human-error aspect of cytology could somehow be removed.

The last reason why smears can be falsely negative is the most puzzling. It seems that while one cervix sheds cells easily, another does not. Maybe a cervix with only a mild abnormality is less likely to shed cells than one which has a more severe abnormality. This is not unreasonable, since, as we saw in Chapter 2, there will be a greater thickness of cells involved the higher the degree of abnormality, so it should be easier to dislodge a few. However, it is known that a cervix which has already developed cancer may also give a negative smear. This aspect is probably beyond our control.

The bottom line is that single smear results, taken in isolation, are not always reliable. However, it is very unlikely that a succession of negative smears taken from the same woman will all be false negatives. This is the explanation of the paradox we encountered earlier: cervical cancer takes around ten years to develop, but relatively frequent smears are required to give the maximum protection against it. If a woman is having yearly smears, an occasional false negative result does not matter: she will have an accurate result within a year or two, which should be well in time to show up an abnormality before it becomes a cancer. However, if the same woman is having a smear only once every five years, the situation is quite different. If she has a false negative smear, there is then a ten-year gap between her last real negative smear and the date her next smear is due. This is too long, and she may then find that she does have cancer, despite having had a 'negative' smear within the last five years.

OK, so why does the government tell you that you can only have a smear every five years? Because it is being advised by people who consider the global view. It is quite definitely true that in countries like Finland, where screening is done only once every five years, there has been a considerable reduction in the incidence of cervical cancer. Take a look at the table below.

This table shows you that screening every three years, on a national level, gives almost the same level of protection as screening every year (a reduction in risk of 91 per cent as opposed to 93 per cent). Even five-yearly screening gives an 83 per cent reduction in risk. But look again at the last column in the table, which shows how many smears each woman would have to have. If your screening programme works on a three-yearly basis, you need only ten smears per woman, as opposed to thirty if they were done yearly. And you get an extra reduction in risk of only two per cent for your twenty extra smears per woman. Financially, I think you have to admit, it makes sense for a country to run a three-yearly screening programme. In fact, there are those who will argue that five-yearly screening makes

Screening frequency (in years)	% reduction in risk	Number of tests (35–64 age range)
1	93.3	30
2	93.3	15
3	91.4	10
5	83.9	6
10	64.2	3

Adapted from IARC 1986, BMJ 293: 659–664

just about as much sense, but the general consensus in the medical profession has been to advise three-yearly screening programmes. Indeed, those are the guidelines given by the British Medical Association (BMA). The government has chosen to continue on a five-yearly basis, despite the BMA's advice. This means that your GP may only be paid for taking a smear every five years, and may be positively discouraged (or even prevented) from taking them more frequently.

So the government says you can have a smear only every five years, the BMA says you should have one every three years, and the figures show that you will be best protected by having a smear every year. Before you write letters of protest, let's sit back and think for a minute. Screening programmes are very, very costly to run and financial decisions have to be made. A yearly screening programme would be ruinously expensive and really wouldn't save many extra lives compared to a three-yearly programme. Although in many countries women are advised to have yearly smears, they nearly always have to pay for those smears themselves, or have them done through insurance schemes. I cannot think of any country which runs a free yearly screening programme.

It therefore seems to me that at present we cannot expect the government to fund a screening programme running on more than a three-yearly basis. We should, however, expect better than the five-yearly programme we have now.

There are groups of women who need more frequent screening anyway, and who should be allowed this within the screening programme. These are women who have already had an abnormal smear or, once the tests are more widely available, those who have a high-risk type HPV (wart virus) infection (see Chapter 8).

These women should have yearly smears. At present HPV typing is not generally available, so it may be that we should screen women more frequently even if they just have a history of wart virus infection, either as genital warts, or seen on a cervical smear. Opinions are divided on this issue at present (see Chapter 8). Another group that I think should have more frequent screening is smokers, since we have seen they are also at higher than average risk, though this is not policy at present.

Another vexed question is: when should women start having smears? Again, various figures are bandied about – at the age of 35, the age of 25, at 20, after the first pregnancy ... basically, the age is not that important. What matters is when a woman starts having sex. She should have her first smear about three years later. So, if she starts having sex at 14, she should have a smear at 17. If she starts at the age of 24, she should have a smear when she is 27. At present, the government guidelines state that women should have smears within the screening programme from the age of 20. This means that a woman who is still a virgin may be pressurised into a smear she does not need (because GPs now have to meet screening targets), while one who has already been sexually active for six years may be told she is not eligible.

It is certainly true that cervical cancer is still uncommon in women under 35, and almost non-existent in women under 20. However, this is where doctors who have to see patients, and statisticians who sit at computers, usually get into fights. Statisticians will tell you that what matters is reducing the number of deaths from cancer, and young women are just not dying of cancer. However, those of us who have the painful task of breaking bad news to young women do not see it the

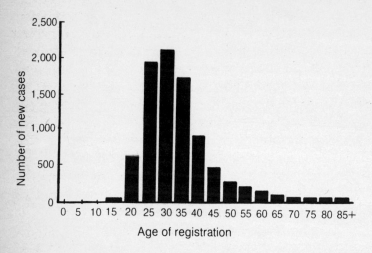

Number of new cases of CIN 3 by age – England and Wales 1984, (OPCS)

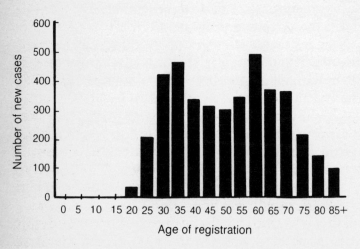

Number of new cases of invasive cervical cancer by age – England and Wales 1984, (OPCS)

same way. Look at the two tables on page 164.

You will see from the second table that quite a substantial number of women are found to have invasive cancer at the age of 30, even at 25. And from the first table you can see that the peak age for CIN 3 is 30, with almost the same number of women being diagnosed at the age of 25. Even at the age of 20, a fair number of women have CIN 3, more than at the age of 45. The statisticians will argue: so what, they won't die of cancer. But there is a world of difference between having CIN 3, or early cancer at the age of 20, or 25, and having the same at 40 or 45. A woman of 40 who is told she needs a cone biopsy or even a hysterectomy will be upset, but at least the chances are she has had children by then. The same is not true for a woman of 20, 25, or even 30, who may not yet have started a family and finds she is denied the possibility of doing so. These women do not end up in the statistical tables for deaths from cancer: they certainly survive, but at a price.

The same arguments about prevention of cancer, not CIN 3, come up in the debate about the frequency of screening. You will always find that statisticians argue the case for longer screening intervals, while those of us at the coal-face want shorter screening intervals. The reasons are exactly the same as I have just described. If I never had to see another young woman (or any woman, for that matter) break down in tears on being told she needs a cone biopsy or a hysterectomy, it wouldn't be too soon.

However, statisticians are good for us doctors, too. They help put things in perspective, precisely because they are not emotionally involved. So the arguments between both groups, doctors and statisticians, are probably a good thing overall; they keep us all thinking and on our toes.

So what should you, as a woman, do about having smears? First of all, make sure you are getting your share of the screening programme. Why miss out on the offer of a free smear? Some women think they can only have their smear with their GP, and are embarrassed to do so, especially if he is male and has known them since childhood. But you are entitled to have your screening smear with other doctors. Your GP may have a female partner or a nurse who could do your smear. If not, you can go to another GP, with whom you are not registered, just for a smear. Or you can go to a family-planning or well-woman clinic. As long as your GP receives a copy of the smear result, it will still count towards his target, that is, the number of women in his practice who have to have a smear before he can receive payment. Family-planning clinics do not usually require a letter from your GP before they will do a smear, you can make your own appointment.

You can also go for smears to a department of genito-urinary medicine (GUM) or a sexually transmitted disease (STD) clinic. These have the advantage of anonymity: they will not send the result to your GP if you so request; and if you are very worried for some reason (for example, you combine the smear with tests for infection and are worried about disclosure), there is nothing to stop you giving a false name. When I worked in a clinic like this, it was quite amusing to see people trying to remember which name they had given, so make sure you keep a note! STD clinics are also more likely to give you yearly smears if you have a history of wart or herpes virus infections, if you have difficulty obtaining them elsewhere.

What if your area allows you only to have a smear every five years? Well, I'm going to stick my neck out here and say that I think it's unfair for some women to be put at greater risk just because of the area they live in, when another health district nearby may be offering three-yearly screening. The first thing to do is to see whether your GP or a clinic will do it anyway – many will, because they feel the same way I do. Sometimes they are prevented from doing so by the cytology laboratory: the smear may be sent back if the lab checks its computer and finds you have had a smear within the last five years. If that is the case, don't blame your doctor, he or she is probably just as annoyed as you are.

Obviously, you can pay to have a smear done, if you can afford it, but in this case, I think it is unfair: three-yearly screening should be a right, not something dependent on your finances or the health district in which you live. I have known women use various devious ways of getting a smear under such circumstances; an obvious one is simply to go to an STD clinic as I have already mentioned. Another way is to take advantage of the ridiculous fact that computers in different health districts do not talk to each other. So, if you have had a smear in one health district, the neighbouring district will not know about it. All you have to do is go to a clinic or a GP in the neighbouring district, though you may need to use a friend's address for the results. These solutions are not entirely honest, and it is a shame that women have had to resort to them. It would be a lot better for all concerned if three-yearly screening was simply the rule for all districts.

What if you want to have more frequent smears? I would suggest that since you can have a free smear every three years, a reasonable option would perhaps be to pay for one in between. That way, you will be having smears at 18-month intervals, which will offer you a high level of protection, but you will be paying for yourself only every three years. If you ask around, you should be able to find a private clinic that will do a smear for around £40–50, including the consultation fee. This works out at £15 a year, which you may feel is worth spending. But if this is too much, remember that the free three-yearly screening is still giving you a good level of protection.

I expect some readers will be angry that I can even suggest women should pay for some of their smears. But life is not fair and no government will fund yearly screening – I have shown you why. So I am simply showing what you might do if you want a higher level of protection than the screening programme can give.

WHEN CAN YOU STOP HAVING SMEARS?

The current government guidelines are that women should have smears until the age of 65. This seems quite reasonable: as we have seen, CIN is more common in younger women, so provided you have had regular smears up till then, it is not very likely that you will develop cervical cancer after you have retired. Although women over 65 do get cervical cancer, the vast majority have never had a smear, or have had inadequate screening. Indeed, an analysis in Scotland in 1993 led doctors there to suggest that women who had been having regular, negative smears could stop having tests at 50. More evidence is still needed that this is safe, so for the time being, I suggest you carry on until you are 65.

There have also been suggestions that women should have tests even later in life. This is certainly true if you have never had a smear, or have not had one for a long time. However, if you have had regular smears and they have been negative, I feel the disadvantages outweigh the advantages. Having smears in your late sixties and seventies is often increasingly uncomfortable, especially if you are not taking hormone replacement therapy. The vagina becomes less elastic, so opening the speculum is more difficult and can be very painful. In addition, the smears can be more difficult to interpret, because as the cells lose the hormone oestrogen, they shrink and tend to look a little like abnormal cells.

What if you have had a hysterectomy (removal of the uterus, or womb)? If the operation was performed for a problem unrelated to cervical cancer (such as heavy periods or fibroids), you need not have further smears, regardless of your age. However, if the hysterectomy was done because of cervical cancer, you should have yearly vaginal smears for at least the next ten years, and probably for longer.

MAKING SURE YOU GET YOUR SMEAR RESULT

Having gone to all the effort of having a smear done, it must be worth making sure you know what the result is. And yet women often forget when and where they last had a smear. Sometimes they have had a smear during a gynaecological check-up, but are unaware it was done. This may lead to unnecessary duplication of smears, but may also result in a situation where smears are assumed to have been taken when in fact they were not. Some clinics and GPs give women a personalised cervical smear record card (see page 170) so that she can record the date and result of her last smear. If they don't, you could create such a page in your diary.

In the last few years there has been considerable publicity regarding women who, for one reason or another, did not receive their smear results: because of this, they did not have follow-up checks and subse-

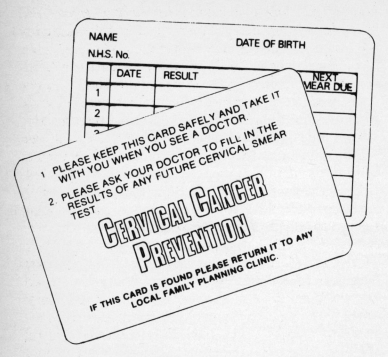

Cervical smear record card

quently died of cancer. Mistakes are always going to happen. You are supposed to be informed of your result, even if it is negative. However, this system will break down if you are not registered with a GP, if you move, or if the result gets lost in the post. In the end, it is up to you to make sure you find out the result, and remember when you last had a smear. After all, it is your life that may be at risk. It is a mistake to rely on other people to take this responsibility. They may be dealing with thousands of results; you are only interested in one, your own. Who is the more likely to lose it?

Having read this book, you should be in a position to understand what your smear result means. There is nothing to stop you asking to see the report for yourself. Don't get fobbed off by doctors or nurses who tell you it might frighten you: that's why you have devoted the time to finding out what the form means. And if there is something on it that you don't understand, well, they will just have to explain it. That is what they are there for. I have personally seen women who thought their last smear was negative, and yet when I obtained a copy, I saw it showed abnormal cells.

I'm not saying you should be on the phone to your doctor within a week of having a smear. Ask how long the results usually take, allow a couple of weeks' grace for inefficiency, postal delays and so on, and make a note in your diary of when to check if you have not been notified. Sometimes it is helpful to leave a stamped addressed envelope in your records. Or, if you know you are coming back for an appointment anyway in the next few months, check then. Even if you leave it till your next six-monthly family-planning appointment – which is likely to be perfectly safe – ask, in case the result has been filed and forgotten, or never came back from the lab.

'In 1984, I went for a routine smear. My life was very busy, I was working hard, travelling a lot. I guess I forgot about the smear really, I just assumed that since I hadn't heard it must be OK. A year later I had some discharge and went to the doctor, a different one as I had moved again. She didn't have my records yet, so she did a smear anyway, since I couldn't remember exactly how long it was since I'd had one. A month later I was posted to the States for a year. In the excitement, I forgot to let the clinic know – well, you tell your friends and your family,

but you can't remember everything. When I came back from the States, I was a bit worried as I'd had some funny bleeding every now and again. I hadn't wanted to see anyone in the States: it was expensive and I thought there was no point since I'd be back home soon. I found a flat in the same area as before, so I went to the doctor I'd seen for the last smear. She was frantic. Hadn't I got the letter a year ago? It turned out that not only the smear she had done, but the one before that were both abnormal. She referred me to the hospital straight away, but it was too late. I had cancer. I had to have a hysterectomy and radiotherapy afterwards. I was 34 then, now I'm 36. It's taken me a long time to come to terms with it, I'm not sure I have yet. People my age don't get cancer. It's not fair.'

I have embellished the details a little, but this was a true story. Don't let it be yours.

10

Emotional feelings and reactions

One of the prerequisites of screening is that the process should not cause psychological harm to those involved. For a long time, this aspect was ignored with regard to cervical screening. After all, here was a test which could actually *prevent* women developing cancer; it was one of the most wonderful advances in medicine. It was unthinkable that it could cause harm. Surely women would be overjoyed at this protection they were getting?

In the last decade, however, it has been increasingly realised that women do in fact suffer emotionally as a result of the whole screening and treatment process. Whereas, previously, research concentrated on purely physical aspects, in recent years a number of studies have been carried out to look at the psychological effects of screening, colposcopy and treatment. You will find details of a couple of books written specifically on this subject in the Further Reading section.

The one thing that emerges as the most important

cause of anxiety is lack of information and understanding as to why smears are taken and what it means
if they are abnormal. This is not new: 'ignorance breeds
fear' is an old saying. The other big problems are the
embarrassment of the procedures involved and the
association of cervical cancer with sexual behaviour.

DECIDING TO HAVE A SMEAR

*'Yes, I meant to have a smear test. I kept meaning to
go. But I always had a reason I couldn't: I was too
busy, it was the wrong time of the month, I wasn't
feeling up to it.'*

*'The thought of the examination put me off. So un-
dignified, I couldn't have such a thing done by a man.'*

Even the decision to go for a smear is not an easy one.
The examination is embarrassing and many women do
not realise that they can insist on seeing a female doctor,
even at another practice or clinic, for a smear.

*'Why should I have a smear? There's nothing wrong
with me. I'll just be wasting the doctor's time.'*

*'It's a test for cancer, isn't it? Well, I'd rather not
know – once you get cancer you're dead.'*

The commonest misconception is that smears test for
cancer, which, as we have seen, is just not true. The
whole point of smears is to pick up changes in cells,
CIN, which are not cancer and which can be completely removed before they ever get the chance to
become cancer.
Again, women think that they don't need tests

because they are well. But the idea is to detect CIN before it ever becomes so serious as to turn into cancer and produce symptoms. Indeed, women are often worried when they have a discharge or bleeding, but actually there is only a small chance that these problems will turn out to be related to cervical cancer or CIN. A discharge is much more likely to be caused by infection. Bleeding after sex can be a sign of cervical cancer, but is much more commonly caused by a cervical ectropion or erosion (see page 43).

'Why should I have a smear? I've only slept with one man, my husband.'

As we have seen, although there is an association between women's sexual behaviour and cervical cancer, the behaviour of the man is equally important. So, although a woman may have been faithful, her partner may place her at risk. It is also important to remember that there are other factors involved, not just sexual behaviour. We know that smoking is likely to be involved, that the immune system is important, but there are still plenty of things we do not know. Sexual behaviour is not the only factor, there may be something else, something we have not suspected, which plays a vital part.

'I'm too old. I haven't had sex for years and years.'

Age is unimportant, so is when you last had sex. If you have not had regular smears, you should still have one, even if you are 70. Many women think that once they have passed through the menopause, the womb no longer has a function and nothing else will happen 'down there'. This is not true.

THE SMEAR TEST ITSELF

It is unfortunate if, having psyched yourself up to have a smear, the examination turns out to be unpleasant. Not only is this traumatic at the time, but it will sour your attitude to future tests, and may put you off altogether. But most women find that the examination is not as bad as they expected and are relieved to find how quick and simple it was. You can do quite a lot to help yourself, by trying to be as relaxed as possible both before and during the examination. Don't choose to have your smear on the same day as a stressful meeting at work. Bring a friend along if you think it will help. Do some relaxation exercises, have a stiff drink; some women get themselves into such a state they need tranquillisers.

If they have not already done so, ask the doctor or nurse to warm the speculum, for example under the hot tap. A freezing-cold metal instrument is no fun at all. If there is an observer in the room, for example a student, remember that you are at liberty to ask for them to leave. They need to learn, but if you are very tense, your needs come first. It is likely that there will be a curtain round the couch, but if there is not (and even if there is, if it will make you feel better), ask for the door to be locked. Having a smear only takes a minute, but if you are worried about someone coming in, even a nurse, it will make the process more difficult.

If there is a reason why you are particularly nervous (for example a bad previous experience, a sexual assault in the past) mention it at the start. Although everyone should be treated with care, it will alert the doctor or nurse to take more time and to be aware that the examination may be difficult.

Once you have had the smear, make sure you find

out what the result was. I have discussed the importance of this in Chapter 9.

AN ABNORMAL, 'POSITIVE' SMEAR RESULT

You are a perfectly rational woman. You have a
responsible position, a career, a family to look after.
Normally you are a rock. You receive a letter which
says, 'Your cervical smear test showed an abnormality.
Please make an appointment to discuss this at your
earliest convenience.' In an instant you turn into a
gibbering wreck.

> *'I just thought, I'm going to die. I went numb, I
> couldn't move. I stood there holding the letter and
> crying.'*

> *'Yes, I went regularly for smears, but I never thought
> I'd have anything wrong. I thought the smear
> protected you.'*

> *'I made the mistake of phoning my mother. She
> made it worse, she started to cry on the phone,
> saying she couldn't believe she was going to lose her
> only daughter.'*

> *'Why me, what did I do?'*

A reaction combining shock, disbelief, guilt and
anger is very common. Some women remain calm, but
they are in a minority. The reaction is mostly due to the
fear of cancer, even in women who, under normal
cirumstances know that an abnormal smear does not
mean cancer. Even nurses and doctors, who are well
informed, can be frightened, deep down.

'*I was devastated. Robert and I had been together for four years and we had just told our parents we were going to get married and start a family. My first thought was that I'd never have children.*'

As we have seen, the treatments for CIN do not affect your fertility. However, many women do not realise this and it is a major source of anxiety.

'*After the initial shock, I started thinking, Why did it happen to me? I haven't been promiscuous. What will John say? What will he think? I remembered I'd had a fling just once during our marriage. It was only one night, after a dinner, when I was away on a course. I'd never mentioned it to John. I felt terrible. Maybe it was all my fault, maybe this was my punishment.*'

Some women blame themselves, others turn on their partner. Did he pass on the wart virus, is he the one to blame? This, in turn may make him feel guilty and rejected. Relationships can suffer at this time because of accusations in both directions and most likely all unnecessary.

A supportive partner can be a great help at this time: remember that he will be worried, even if he is not showing it. Many men do feel guilty, even without being reminded. Newspapers and magazines have spread the word about the 'high-risk male' quite widely. Men are often seen in sexually transmitted disease clinics asking to be checked for warts in case they might infect their girlfriends or wives. It is very frustrating for them to be told that there is no way they can be given an unconditional all-clear – there is always the possibility of microscopic infection, for which nothing can be done. Unfortunately, some men go along looking for confirmation that they have no visible warts; if this is given, without the caution that there might be microscopic infection, they may go home and accuse their partner of being unfaithful, or tell her it must be her fault. Accusations from either partner are only hurtful and achieve nothing positive. It is far more useful for both partners to realise each other's fears and guilt and help each other through the experience.

The most important thing to do if you are informed of an abnormal smear is to discuss it fully with your doctor. Some doctors are better informed than others: if yours cannot give you the information you need, read as much as you can find on the subject. Talk to other women who have been through the experience already – only remember that their result may not have been the same as yours, so not everything they say may be applicable to you.

It is worth mentioning that some women and their partners are worried that continuing to have sex might make the abnormal cells get worse. This is not the case: indeed, you really should make the most of your time, because if you have to have treatment, you will be advised to abstain for a month afterwards!

AT THE COLPOSCOPY CLINIC

In theory, if women attending colposcopy clinics were fully informed about the meaning of their smear results, they should not be anxious. However, even informed women often experience anxiety at the thought of the examination and what might be found.

Many women find the wait between the smear result and a colposcopy very stressful, especially if it takes several months. It is always worth asking your GP if another hospital has a shorter waiting list – but check why: maybe it has a bad reputation! You can use the time constructively. Find out as much as you can about the procedure, the possible treatments, particularly about what is likely to be on offer at the hospital you are going to attend. Check whether you might be offered treatment on the same day as your initial examination, in the so-called 'See and Treat' clinics. These are discussed in detail in Chapter 4. The main practical implication for you is that you may need to make extra arrangements at home and work if you have treatment that day. Nowadays there are support groups in some areas, run by women who have gone through the experience of an abnormal smear. See if there is a local one you could go to.

If you are a smoker, maybe this could provide that final incentive to give up. However, do bear in mind that stopping smoking may be an additional cause of stress at a time when you are already tense and worried.

> '*During the weeks before my appointment, I read all the books and leaflets I could get hold of. Some of them contradicted each other, which was confusing. As I went along, I wrote down questions about things I didn't understand, or which didn't seem to be answered by the books. Then, before I went to the hospital, I made a list of the questions I felt I should ask. Normally, I find I clam up when I'm faced with a doctor in a white coat. Having a list made it a lot easier.*'

Many doctors find it easier to answer questions than to think of things to say on their own, so don't be afraid to ask. Some questions may need to wait until after the examination, as the doctor will not know what is actually wrong with you until then.

The position you have to lie in during the colposcopy examination can be described, at best, as inelegant. Once again, relaxation is important, especially as the procedure will take longer than a smear. Do not hesitate to ask for privacy (for example by having the door locked): in some clinics doctors and nurses just wander in and out of the rooms without warning. They may be used to women lying with their legs in the air but you are not; they know who they are, but as far as you are concerned, they could be Joe Bloggs from the newspaper shop. The same applies to observers: they should be introduced to you first, and your permission requested for them to stay.

It is sometimes said that once you have had a baby you can never be embarrassed again. This is not true. For a start, having a baby is (one hopes) an experience which is expected to have a pleasant and rewarding outcome. Women therefore approach it in quite a different manner and perceive it differently. In addition, they are often so tired and so glad to get it over with that they have ceased to care about elegance and privacy. Lastly, the memory of the actual labour and delivery, like many painful and unpleasant experiences, fades, and therefore cannot be readily drawn on for comparison. So do not let yourself be made to feel inadequate by this kind of statement, even though it may be well meant.

> '*I was so nervous before – and during the examination, for that matter. But afterwards, I was so relieved. At least I knew what was going on and that it wasn't cancer.*'

Most women feel much happier after their colposcopy, because the uncertainty has been removed.
Make sure before you leave that you have asked all the
questions you wanted to. It often helps to have your
partner or a friend present because you may not be able
remember everything. I have often found myself repeating things several times within one consultation,
because it is obvious that my patient has not taken in
what I have said. It has occasionally been suggested
that such conversations are taped, to be listened to
later, but I think some doctors would find that daunting and might be less open and helpful – not necessarily
consciously but just through 'stage fright'.

If you have not seen it in a book or a leaflet, take the
opportunity to get the doctor to draw you a picture of
your cervix, or show you a photograph, if that is
possible. Many women seem to have the idea that the
abnormal area is somehow mouldy, or fungating, or a
black hole. It makes everything much less frightening if
you know what it really looks like. This is one of the
advantages of cervicography, a technique of photo-
graphing the cervix, which I shall be discussing in the
next chapter.

Unfortunately, the colposcopy is usually followed by
another period of waiting and anxiety, before the
biopsy result comes back. You may be given another
appointment for this, or, more often, you will be
informed by letter. This is why it is so important that
you have thought through and discussed all the options
by the end of your colposcopy visit: you may not easily
have another chance to talk to the specialist until your
treatment or next colposcopy appointment. If you do
find you have been taken by surprise, do not be
frightened of asking for another appointment to discuss it again. It is very unlikely you would be refused;

most doctors working in this field know how anxious women become and will be sympathetic.

TREATMENT

Although some clinics treat women at the same visit as the initial colposcopy, it is more common to have the treatment performed at a separate visit. You may see this as an advantage, a chance to prepare yourself and learn more about the problem. However, the waiting can make some women very anxious. Relationships with families and friends suffer because you are tense and irritable, your performance at work declines and so on. Do not struggle on by yourself, counselling may help.

Most women are pleasantly surprised and relieved once they have had their treatment. It is not nearly as painful or traumatic as they expected. However, the thought that part of their cervix has had to be destroyed leaves some women with psychological and psychosexual problems. A study has been done which compared women who had abnormal smears with those who had come into contact with a sexually transmitted disease, non-specific urethritis (chlamydia). The study looked at features such as interest in sex, feelings towards the partner, pain during sex and satisfaction with sex. Women who had an abnormal smear necessitating colposcopy and treatment were found to have far more negative feelings towards sex than those women who knew their partners had non-specific urethritis and who were treated for it themselves.

Interestingly, women who knew their partners had penile warts, but who themselves had a normal cervical smear, did not react in this way. Although they knew they had come into contact with a risk factor, and the connotations were presumably much the same, psychologically they did not seem to be affected any more than were women whose partners had non-specific urethritis.

It is also interesting that the abnormal smear itself did not seem to be associated with psychosexual problems. No change in attitude was noted from the time the women knew their smear was abnormal to the time they had their colposcopy, even though, in many cases, this interval amounted to several months. However, their attitudes changed significantly *after* they had had colposcopy and treatment. They showed loss of interest in sex, felt hostile towards their partner, did not enjoy sex as much as before, and often said they experienced pain during intercourse.

Of course, these feelings are often related to one another, and may be related most of all to the woman's anxiety. For example, a woman who is feeling anxious about her cervix may well be worried about having sex. She is therefore not very relaxed during intercourse and does not find the experience as pleasant and satisfying as she did before. Anxiety about her sexual performance may then be added to her other worries. Her partner may feel rejected and the relationship may suffer. When she has sex again, she will be even more anxious than before, will thus be more tense, find it more uncomfortable and the experience will be even less pleasant for both partners. A vicious circle soon develops, as a result of which she is likely to feel that it is preferable not to have sex at all and avoid the issue altogether.

'I found it really hard to have sex. On one hand I was frightened of losing Richard and adding to my problems. On the other, the last thing I was inter-

ested in was doing something which constantly reminded me of the abnormality.'

The results of this study are worrying. More and more young women are developing CIN: they may not yet have found a stable relationship or started their family. It would appear that they may be placed at a considerable disadvantage in future relationships, and may develop a variety of psychosexual problems which could both hinder the formation of a relationship or harm an existing one.

'It wasn't so bad before the colposcopy: I suppose I kept hoping it could be a mistake, maybe there was nothing wrong with me after all. But once the doctor said he could see an abnormal area on my cervix I knew it was true. I went home and cried. I didn't have a boyfriend, he'd cheated on me and we'd split up the year before. I felt really sorry for myself. No one would ever want me now, I was dirty, maybe I was infectious, I had a disease. I felt like a leper. When I split up with Joe, I was angry, I knew he'd mistreated me. Suddenly I felt, maybe he'd been right, I was worthless.'

These women and their partners need help. In recognition of this, some colposcopy units have set up counselling services, but they are still in a minority. It could be argued that counselling should become a routine part of the whole treatment process: prevention is better than cure. More doctors are now aware of the problem and try to make gentle enquiries as to how things are going. Sometimes all that is needed is to clear up a misunderstanding or answer a lack of information. If the problem is deeper, specialised counselling

will be needed. You will find some addresses at the back
of this book, and your clinic or GP may be able to give
you further advice. A women's support group may be
another useful source of help and information: sharing
feelings and realising that other people also have them
is often helpful.

'Peter didn't seem particularly concerned at first, but I
noticed he became more reserved. He still touched me
and kissed me, but he'd always make excuses so that
we didn't actually have sex. After the treatment we
were told not to, anyway, but the month went past and
he made no moves. I was a bit embarrassed to talk
about it, I was having trouble coming to terms with
the whole thing myself anyway. By the time I went for
my check-up this had been going on for months.
Luckily, I saw the same doctor as before. I decided to
mention it. She asked if Peter had come with me: he
was sitting outside. She called him in and had a
general chat with both of us, stressing how sex
couldn't harm me and that very few women had
problems again in their lives after treatment. Peter
asked specifically about that again during the con-
versation, and then said he'd been so worried that he
might make the condition come back by having sex
with me. The reassurance did the trick.'

CANCER

There can be few pieces of news which are worse to
give or receive than a diagnosis of cancer. The person
receiving it sees before them a bleak future of pain and
suffering followed by death. The person giving it
knows this and feels a mixture of sympathy, sorrow,
and even guilt, as though it were somehow their fault

and that it is in some way unfair that they themselves are healthy. The family of the affected person will also have feelings of guilt, of sorrow and of helplessness. Sometimes this helplessness turns into hostility directed at the person giving the news, or even towards the woman herself. A great deal of understanding on all sides is therefore required at such a difficult time.

> *'I felt helpless, devastated. I didn't know what to do, I heard the doctor say "cancer" and I just froze. I couldn't think of anything to ask. I just sat there.'*

> *'The only thing I could think about was, Who's going to look after Jimmy and Kim? I won't see them grow up, I won't see them go to school, get married, nothing.'*

A great deal may be said at the time the diagnosis is given, but it is unlikely that you or your family would take much in. It is therefore important to have a second appointment, fairly soon after the first, at which the whole issue can be discussed again. By this time, it is likely that you will have plenty of questions to ask.

It is worth bearing in mind, if you find yourself in this unhappy position, that the doctor who sees you is only a human being. It is very unlikely he or she has had any training in counselling techniques; it is somehow expected that these will be 'picked up' on the way. The doctor may therefore be feeling very awkward and may not really know what to say or how to say it, despite wanting to be as sympathetic and helpful as possible. Do not be inhibited from asking questions: this is a good time to do so.

Once again, the association of cervical cancer with sex makes some women feel guilty. This is often particularly marked in women who have had abortions or extramarital affairs. They may feel they are being punished for what they have done 'wrong'. Young women, who have not had children, may feel both cheated and punished, and may have strong feelings of both guilt and resentment.

> '*I was so angry with myself. I knew I should have gone for a smear earlier, but I just kept putting it off. Really, I had no one but myself to blame.*'

> '*My husband was awful. He kept saying, "You silly woman, why didn't you have the smear done when you were supposed to? Now see what's happened." I knew it was really that he was so upset, but he made it much worse for me.*'

Women who feel they 'got what they deserve' often become deceptively good, compliant patients, as if they feel they may get a reprieve for good behaviour. This is a mistake, as deep feelings of anger, resentment and fear may be suppressed. Such bargaining is likely to lead only to disappointment and further psychological problems; counselling is a much better solution.

HYSTERECTOMY

The treatment of cancer often requires a hysterectomy (removal of the womb, or uterus). Many women, even if they have completed their family, find this daunting and disturbing. The uterus is often perceived as the essence of a woman's femininity; without it she may feel she is no longer a complete woman. Also, periods are sometimes felt to be a cleansing of the system, without which poisons of some kind will accumulate in the body.

'It felt strange, the idea of having my womb removed. In one way, the thought of not having periods and not needing contraception any more was good; but more often I found it frightening.'

What you have to remember is that the womb is nothing more than a box in which to hold a baby. It has no other function. The blood which is shed each month is only the lining of the womb, which has thickened during the cycle in preparation for a fertilised egg which never materialised. Periods have no other meaning or function.

'I thought, My husband will start looking around, I'll be like an old woman.'

The ovaries are not usually removed, unless you are approaching the menopause anyway. Even if they are removed, you can use hormone replacement therapy to help keep you looking and feeling 'young and beautiful'! It is not possible to go into all the pros and cons of hormone replacement here: obviously you will need to find out more for yourself, but it really is helpful for the majority of women.

Any type of hysterectomy involves a considerable change in a woman's self-image. For a start, she will no longer be capable of having children. There is a world of difference between 'I don't want any (or any more) children' and 'I can't have any (or any more) children'.

'It was a relief, really, not to worry about contraception any more. We've got two children and that's enough! I'd been wondering whether to have a sterilisation: this solved both problems at once.'

'*I was devastated. True, we had two lovely boys and hadn't been trying for another child. But it had been in the back of my mind that it might be nice to have a little girl. Suddenly, the decision wasn't mine any more.*'

Some women find the idea of sex with no possibility of becoming pregnant difficult. All methods of contraception have a failure rate, no matter how small: this element of risk may be crucial for some women to enjoy sex. They may therefore lose interest in sex after a hysterectomy.

'*I was embarrassed. I thought maybe my husband would notice the difference inside when we had sex. I felt somehow like a freak, an abnormal woman. Although I looked normal to other people, I didn't feel normal myself.*'

'*I was so worried that sex would be no good that I didn't want to try. I thought the longer I could put it off, somehow maybe the problem would go away. My boyfriend was very understanding, but after six months he started suggesting we should talk about it, try it. I found it very hard.*'

Many women worry that they will not be able to have sex normally after their operation. This can, of course, become a self-fulfilling prophecy, as the anxiety interferes with their sexual desire, their enjoyment and so on.

In fact a hysterectomy should, in theory, make little or no difference to a woman's life, including her sex life. During the weeks following the operation you are bound to feel tired and weak. Many women say it takes two, even three months before they feel themselves again. However, it is important to try to resume sexual activity sooner rather than later; the later you leave it, the more likely you are to experience difficulty when restarting. Don't feel a failure if you need to use lubricants: anxiety affects your lubrication, and you are bound to feel anxious at the start. If you allow this situation to become a vicious circle (anxiety, dryness, more anxiety, more dryness), you will not be doing yourself a favour. Perhaps just as importantly, your partner needs to understand that you are not dry because of lack of interest in him, it is the anxiety, uncertainty and embarrassment of your situation.

The role of a supportive partner cannot be emphasised enough. Several studies and surveys have shown that women in long-term stable relationships fare much better than single women or those in unstable relationships. Indeed, women who are young and not in a relationship generally find it very difficult to start a new relationship afterwards. A partner can do a great deal to allay fears of rejection, unattractiveness and loss of femininity. Even when actual intercourse is impossible, he can show his affection in other ways: this maintains a woman's confidence in herself and their relationship.

> 'His reaction was, "It's your problem, I'm getting out," and that was it. He just left.'

> 'We'd been going through a bad patch and I suppose this was the last straw.'

While a good relationship is positively helpful, an unstable one may collapse under the strain of illness and suffering. Similarly, women who tend towards depression and anxiety in normal life are more likely to suffer after the operation.

'It was odd: I was so strong throughout all the treatment. Everyone remarked on how determined I was. And yet when they finally told me I was OK, I fell apart.'

'I'd given up everything else in my life to concentrate on surviving. It was my only goal. When I was told I was cured, I thought, What do I do now?'

Sometimes, even being pronounced cured can be stressful. Having channelled every ounce of strength and emotion into coping with cancer, it can be difficult to readjust to being a normal, healthy person. Again, understanding from family and friends is important in making the adjustment successfully. Some women have found it helpful to run a support group for others, or to help with one: passing on your experiences can be useful therapy for all concerned.

RADIOTHERAPY

Many people are frightened of radiation and therefore fear this treatment almost as much as the disease itself. The fact that the treatment goes on for several weeks and is often accompanied by ill-health does not help in coping with it emotionally. It is very important to have enough time to discuss your fears and worries about side effects with the consultant.

Unfortunately, radiotherapy causes the tissues in the pelvis to fibrose (stiffen) and this does often lead to problems during sex. Advice is needed as to comfortable positions: the most successful are likely to be those in which deep penetration does not occur, at least initially. Radiotherapy also interferes with the function of the ovaries, resulting in a lack of oestrogen. Again, hormone replacement therapy is very useful: not only does it help psychologically and symptomatically, it also helps in the healing of the tissues.

There is another side effect during treatment: women may notice vaginal discharge and bleeding, especially after intercourse. This is particularly alarming, as these are likely to be the very symptoms which led to the diagnosis of cancer. It is important to understand that they are simply a side effect, and not signs of things getting worse.

Some people think that they become dangerous to others while receiving radiotherapy, which may add to negative feelings they already have about themselves. It is only true, and then only for a short time, if a source of radiation is actually placed within the body. It certainly does not apply to external radiation treatment: you do not glow in the dark afterwards.

'I wish they could just have done an operation: all this toing and froing and never feeling well, it's wearing me down.'

Radiotherapy is often viewed with disappointment compared to surgery – it is nicer to feel that the cancer has been cut out and taken away. This is not the case with radiotherapy, but it is important to remember that it can still result in a cure.

RADICAL SURGERY AND CHEMOTHERAPY

These really are outside the scope of this book. Both forms of treatment are a last resort and it is not surprising, therefore, that women who receive them are likely to be depressed and anxious. As always, counselling is very important in helping women and their familes cope. Comprehensive information about what to expect and what can be done about side effects is essential.

FINALLY

While reading this chapter, you may once or twice have thought, 'Surely sex is the last thing on any woman's mind when she is ill, may even have cancer?' That is certainly true initially, when a woman is mostly concentrating on fighting the illness and being cured. But 95 per cent of women with CIN are cured after the first treatment. Even those unfortunate enough to have early cancer still have a reasonable chance of cure. Life then has to go on.

The association of cervical cancer with sex makes it almost inevitable that women will be thinking about sex and relationships, even if the physical side is not currently an issue. Indeed, you may start to review your whole attitude to life and love. Some women ultimately find it a positive experience:

> '*I sat down and thought about my life. What a waste, I was just drifting. I wasn't being stretched in my job, Peter and I had long just been coexisting. I hadn't faced up to any of these things. I think the feeling that I might die (even though rationally I knew I didn't have cancer) made me want to change my life, do something useful with it.*'

In March 1989, the *Lancet*, a leading medical journal, published excerpts from a letter it had received from a doctor who herself had had an abnormal smear. She had suffered a horrific experience. Among many other things: 'The tone of grim satisfaction with which the clinic nurse told me, "That's what comes from sleeping with too many men too young," made me want to hit her.' Her examination was watched by nine or ten male observers: 'That gaggle of men's faces peering down my vagina is not a pleasant memory.' She concludes, 'The memory of the pain, embarrassment and trauma remains, and is re-activated whenever I have the smallest gynaecological problem.'

In the last few years there has been increasing recognition of the emotional toll placed on women by abnormal smears, CIN and cancer. Counselling, once unheard of, is now being introduced into some colposcopy clinics. Lack of funding has limited the progress in this area, but awareness of it has increased nevertheless. I hope that your experience will be an improvement on those of some women in the past.

Some of the emotional difficulties experienced by women and their partners are due to a lack of information or a misunderstanding of the facts. I hope that by reading this you will at least manage to avoid those problems and will have gained some understanding of the emotional processes which may seem bewildering and frightening, but are not uncommon. You are not alone, and there are counsellors and support groups out there: help can be found if you ask.

11

Looking ahead – possibilities for the future

We have seen that the cervical smear is not perfect. It would be nice to have a simple, preferably automated, test which was more accurate. During the last fifteen years, an increasing amount of research has been aimed at improving cervical screening. Inevitably, there have been disappointments, 'breakthroughs' which turned out to be false hopes. For example, you may remember great excitement about the free-radical test, which was later shown to be unreliable and has now been abandoned. In this chapter I shall mention techniques and research which at present appear promising – but any one of them could yet fail to live up to expectations.

CERVICOGRAPHY

Cervicography is already available, but it is used in so few centres in this country that not many women have access to it.

Cervicography is simply a technique for taking

photographs of the cervix without using a colposcope. As we have seen, smears are fraught with problems: they can be taken incorrectly and abnormalities can be missed in the laboratory. They rely heavily on human input and are therefore subject to human error. If only every woman could have a colposcopy instead of a smear – but neither is that practical, nor would all women consider it acceptable. The cost of a colposcopy is enormous relative to that of a smear: after all, a smear can be done by doctors and nurses who are not gynaecologists. Colposcopy can be done only by specially trained doctors. The colposcope itself costs thousands of pounds, not to mention the couch and other accessories. And then, would many women really want to go through the colposcopy examination, which, as we have seen, takes longer and may be considered more embarrassing than a smear?

Taking photographs of the cervix is not a new idea: colpophotography is the name given to the technique of taking photographs through a colposcope. In this case, the camera relies on the lens within the colposcope itself, so it has to be physically attached to a colposcope. It is very difficult to take good photographs in this way. For a start, photographically, most doctors are at the level of the instamatic camera and have no idea what they are doing when faced with problems of magnification and exposure. Not surprisingly, the results are often useless.

The gynaecologist who developed cervicography had trained as a photographer before doing medicine. He realised that what was needed was a simple technique that would enable photographs of the cervix to be taken without using a colposcope. He developed the cerviscope (shown on page 201 and 202).

He started out with an ordinary 35mm SLR camera.

Cerviscope

A special lens was needed to allow photographs to be taken of a small object (namely, the cervix), without having the camera close: you wouldn't want the camera inside you, I'm sure! Then there was the problem of lighting; it is very dark when you look down a speculum. For this reason, the cerviscope has a powerful ring flash for taking the photograph. It also has an ordinary light facility, so that the operator can see what he or she is doing.

Everything possible has been fixed or automated, so that doctors and nurses do not have to make any photographic decisions. The focus range is fixed, so you just move the camera backwards and forwards until the picture looks sharp. There is a considerable leeway allowed on the focusing, so that even if the operator has poor eyesight, the chances are the picture will still be sharp. The exposure control is fully

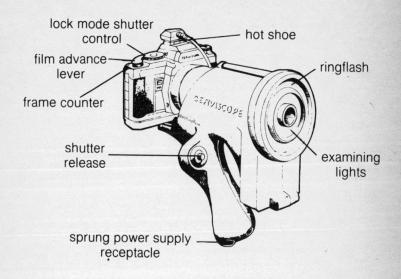

lock mode shutter control

film advance lever

frame counter

shutter release

hot shoe

ringflash

examining lights

sprung power supply receptacle

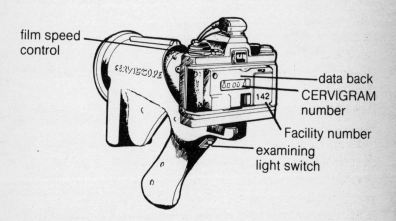

film speed control

data back

CERVIGRAM number

Facility number

examining light switch

The components of a cerviscope

automatic and the film speed is preset. All the person using the camera has to do is switch it on, check they can see the cervix, then press a button.

The procedure for taking a photograph using the cerviscope is much the same as that for a smear. It is preferable to use the same type of couch as for a colposcopy, but it can be done using an ordinary couch. A speculum is inserted and some dilute acetic acid is applied to the cervix, just as in colposcopy. A photograph is taken, and the procedure is repeated to obtain a second picture. Sometimes another photograph may be taken after iodine has been used to stain the cervix, again as in colposcopy. The whole procedure takes just a couple of minutes.

The beauty of this system is that anyone can do it. The only expertise needed is to be able to insert a speculum and see the cervix. Any doctor or nurse who

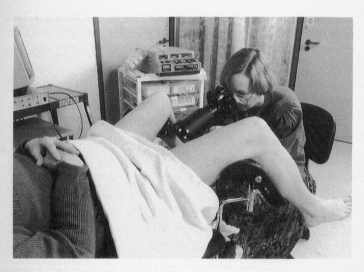

Cervicography being done

takes smears can do cervicography. No expensive colposcope is needed. The photographs, called cervicograms, are taken on slide film and are of the whole cervix. They are sent for evaluation to an expert in colposcopy: when projected on a screen, the magnification is enormous, just as at colposcopy. An expert can study these photographs almost as if doing a colposcopy – but you do not need to be there!

It takes about twenty minutes to do one colposcopy: in that time, an expert can look at ten women's cervicograms. The evaluation (which includes an assessment of the estimated degree of abnormality) is sent back to the clinic, together with a print which can be kept in the woman's records. This serves two functions. First, it means you can see what your cervix looks like, and see any abnormal area. Since women sometimes think an abnormality means something is rotting inside, it can be reassuring to see that it is just a small white patch. Secondly, the picture can be compared with others taken before or afterwards, so any changes can be seen. This type of documentation is an important advantage of cervicography: most of the time, doctors doing a colposcopy draw what they see. However, artistic skills vary, and the accuracy of the drawings can always be called into question. A photograph provides definite evidence of what the cervix looked like at any given time.

Cervicography misses very little, so you are very unlikely to have a false negative result. However, it has the opposite problem: it can give false positive results. In early studies, the false positive rates were very high, which was unacceptable, but over the years, the reporting system has been refined and it is now around 25 per cent. This means that if your cervicogram is reported as abnormal there is a one in four chance it will turn out to be nothing. Why should this happen? In Chapter 4

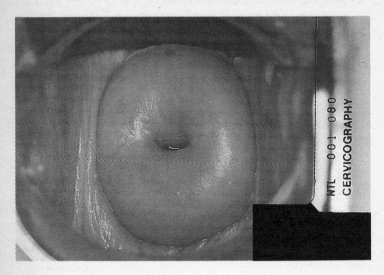

Cervicogram of normal cervix.

White area showing abnormality

Cervicogram showing abnormal area on cervix

I mentioned the problem that not everything which turns white with acetic acid is abnormal. This affects both colposcopy and cervicography. The doctor reporting the cervicogram sees an area which looks aceto-white, or abnormal: the only way to be sure is to take a biopsy, so it must be called 'positive'.

This problem with false positive results is the main reason why cervicography is not suitable for mass screening programmes: the cost of the procedure coupled with an increase in workload for colposcopy clinics would overload the system and is not cost-effective. However, for an individual woman, it can be very reassuring. At least if it is negative, you can be pretty sure it really is negative. And the vast majority of women I have spoken to have said they would rather have a false positive than a false negative result, especially when they have been warned of the possibility in advance.

> 'When I got the letter saying I should have further tests, I wasn't so worried. The doctor had told me if this happened there was a good chance it would turn out to be nothing. Actually, it made me feel better when I went for the colposcopy, because I kept thinking, It'll be a false alarm. In the event, there really was an abnormality, so I was glad I'd had it done.'

At present, if you have cervicography, you will still have a smear at the same time. The basis for this is that a photograph cannot see up the cervical canal, so a small area of abnormality which was totally within the canal could be missed. In practice, this is rare, and a recent study has suggested that virtually no abnormalities, and certainly no serious abnormalities, would be missed by abandoning the concurrent smear. This would cut down the cost of the procedure and has a further advantage: the smear has to be taken before the photographs, because acetic acid affects the quality of smears. Taking the smear may cause a little bleeding, which in turn obscures the view of the cervix and results in a poor-quality cervicogram. These 'technically defective' cervicograms have to be repeated, which is a nuisance for you, as you have to come back and have the examination again.

In any case, the person reporting the cervicogram comments on whether the squamo-columnar junction (see page 24) could be seen. If not, a separate smear is called for, preferably using a Cytobrush, to ensure that the cervical canal is checked. However, this could be done as a separate procedure, for the minority of women who need it. Cervicography is still evolving and it will be interesting to watch for future developments in the technique.

Another possible use for cervicography, and one which may be more acceptable within the NHS, is to investigate women with borderline or mildly abnormal smears. At present, these women are often left to have another smear, or even two smears, before they are called for colposcopy. As we have seen, some of these women should be seen sooner because they already have more severe degrees of abnormality than their smears suggest. Cervicography after the first abnormal smear would help sort out which women need to be seen quickly and which women can safely wait.

Cervicography was first introduced in the United States and has become increasingly popular over there. However, in the US, women have to pay for it. There has been considerable resistance to its use over here, mainly because of the cost implications to an already overstretched service. It seems unlikely that it will ever be used in the NHS screening programme. However, some units have started using it for the evaluation of women with mildly abnormal smears, as mentioned above. Cervicography is available for any woman requesting it at some private screening clinics, mentioned at the end of this book.

AUTOMATED TESTS

By this stage in the book, it has probably become obvious that screening tests are frequently let down by human error. Thus, it would be useful to remove as much as possible of the human element.

Computerised cervical screening is a possibility. A computer can be programmed to recognise a large number of different cell appearances and to identify which ones are normal and which suspicious. This eliminates a tedious feature of laboratory screening, which is checking the 90 per cent of samples that turn out to be normal. By using the computer system, cytologists need only check the samples that are identified as suspicious. Although the equipment is expensive, it should save time and labour, and, in addition, reduce the laboratory false-negative rate.

A test called the HDA (hydrolysed DNA assay test) has been developed which looks specifically at the DNA within the nucleus of the cell. You will recall that each cell contains DNA, the blueprint that dictates how the cell develops and functions (see Chapter 2). If something happens to alter the DNA, the cell will develop in a different, perhaps abnormal, way.

Even conventional cytology testing looks at the nucleus, checking its size relative to the rest of the cell. This new test, however, stains the DNA in a special way and then measures its optical density. It seems that the denser the DNA, the greater the degree of abnormality. An advantage is that only a few cells seem to be required and the test can detect abnormalities even in smears where the cells look normal by conventional cytology: it appears that even very early changes in the DNA are enough to give a positive result.

This method is almost fully automatic. The smear still has to be taken in the conventional way, but is then treated differently in the laboratory. All the laborious staring at cells is done by machine, indeed, just about all the preparation can be done by machine. This means that the test could be quite cheap and quick if done on a large scale.

Preliminary results have been encouraging, with few false negatives or false positives. Refinements still need to be made so that the different degrees of abnormality can be identified more clearly: at present, there is some overlap, so that it is difficult to be sure, for example, if a given result means 'CIN 1' or 'CIN 2'. However, it is to be hoped that work will continue in this area.

TESTING FOR HUMAN PAPILLOMAVIRUS (HPV)

In Chapter 8 we looked at the evidence for the involvement of HPV in cervical cancer. As we saw, there are high-risk types of HPV, whose presence can help to predict which women will have high grades of abnormality. This area is now the subject of intense interest. For some time doctors in the field of colposcopy and screening have been concerned about the amount of over-treatment that must be going on. It is quite impossible that every woman who has CIN 1 will go on to develop cervical cancer. Some early abnormalities must go away on their own, or never progress to anything serious. If only we could predict which they were and leave them alone.

If we could pinpoint which HPV types were the important ones, and have an accurate test for their presence, maybe the problem would be solved. The polymerase chain reaction (PCR) method might allow us to do just that – but there are limitations. It is almost certain that there are still HPV types, some high risk, which have not been identified, even though you would think sixty was already a lot. While that is the case, some women will be missed. Then there is the problem that around five per cent of cervical cancers do not appear to be associated with HPV: they might be associated with unknown types, but it is equally possible that not all cancers are related to HPV. Again, women could be missed.

The PCR technique itself is still being refined and would have to be simplified further to be used in mass screening. This is probably just a matter of time unless some major unexpected problem is encountered. One of the unanswered questions is this: what happens when a woman is found to have a high-risk HPV type, for example HPV 16, but no abnormality can be seen? Is she at higher risk of developing CIN or cancer in the future? Given the evidence to date, one would assume she is. But what happens if the HPV then seems to disappear? Has it really gone, or is it just that the test did not pick it up this time? There is some evidence of occasional fluctuations in HPV testing; tests taken at intervals on the same woman may not always give consistent results. Interestingly, some HPV types seem more prone to this than others, but it is still a grey area.

An interesting observation is that young women (under 30) seem to be more likely to have high-risk

HPV types than older women. Why should this be so? It has been speculated that women are more likely to acquire the virus when young (presumably because of greater sexual activity), but the immune system will fight and get rid of it in many cases. Perhaps those women who still have HPV when they are older are the ones whose immune system for some reason has not been able to cope – for example, because they smoke. If this is the case, then it would be particularly important to screen older women for HPV, as those who were picked up presumably would be at high risk of either already having or developing high grade CIN or even cancer.

More research is needed. Two areas are of particular interest. First, could HPV testing be used to identify women whose smears suggest borderline or mildly abnormal cells but who actually have a higher grade of abnormality? This seems very likely, but needs to be shown in large studies. Secondly, how useful could HPV testing be in screening? Although a small study has shown promise, again larger studies are required. Could we ever abandon the smear and just use HPV testing? This is an attractive idea, as it would be both quicker and cheaper – but much more evidence will be required before such a radical step could safely be taken.

VACCINES

As we have seen, a number of human papillomavirus (HPV) types appear to be strongly associated with cervical cancer. We have vaccines to protect us from other virus infections, for example, rubella (German measles) and smallpox, so why should we not be able

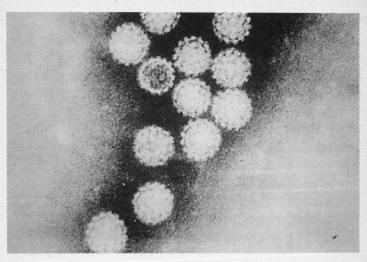

HPV seen through an electron microscope

to apply the same principle to cervical cancer?

There are several problems. First, HPV is a particularly difficult virus to grow artificially: it only likes to reproduce in living cells, and does not respond well to laboratory cell cultures. This means it is difficult to produce enough of it for research studies, let alone start a production line for a vaccine. The second problem is that there are so many HPV types, at least sixty so far. Each type would need its own vaccine. In practice, however, we would not need sixty vaccines. Only about five or six types seem to be strongly associated with cancer, and, of those, HPV 16 and 18 are probably the most important. So it would be possible to have just two vaccines, at least at the start, and still give a significant degree of protection.

Scientists have already been working on HPV vaccines for over ten years, but the end is still not in sight. There are many, many technical problems to overcome.

The first vaccines may not be against types 16 and 18 at all. HPV types 6 and 11, which are the ones in visible genital warts, may act as a testing ground: since they cause a visible problem, it would be easier to see whether the vaccines work. Such vaccines, although not effective against cervical cancer, would in any case be very welcome: genital warts are increasingly common, difficult to treat, unsightly and a cause of much embarrassment. And once these vaccines had been tried and tested, more progress could be made on the potentially life-saving ones.

THE POLARPROBE

The Polarprobe is a completely new concept in the field of cervical screening and diagnosis. It consists of a hand-held pencil-shaped instrument which is made of plastic and is 250 millimetres long and 6 millimetres thick. The probe is inserted into the vagina and moved across the surface of the cervix. It uses a combination of electrical pulses (1.2 volts per 10 milliseconds, at intervals of 0.125 seconds: don't worry, you won't get an electric shock!) and low-intensity light to measure electrical activity and light reflections within cells. Scientists have shown that these are different in normal and abnormal cells. This information is relayed to a laptop computer, to which the probe is attached. Very sophisticated software has been designed to give the computer an enormous memory of normal and abnormal variants. When new signals come in, the computer instantly compares them with the ones it knows and can thus give an assessment of the tissue.

As you can imagine, the system depends on having every single possibility stored in its memory, and this is what researchers have been doing over the last ten years. By 1993, they were confident the probe would be at least 90 per cent accurate, and they embarked on research studies to test it in women. These studies are mainly being carried out in Australia (where the probe was developed), Singapore and the UK. Preliminary results (on relatively few women as yet) show that the probe is almost 100 per cent accurate at detecting invasive cancer, but its sensitivity is not quite as high with low grade abnormalities. Further results are awaited with great interest.

If it fulfils its promise, the Polarprobe has several potential uses. It could be used in colposcopy, to give a more accurate assessment, instantly, of what degree of abnormality is present. As I have discussed, the white appearance which occurs with acetic acid does not always mean there is an abnormality. The probe could perhaps also give an indication of the best place from which to take a biopsy, that is, the place with the highest degree of abnormality. Could it even replace biopsies? Who knows.

The probe could be used in screening, if it was cheap enough. Every surgery and clinic would then have to have one, preferably one in each clinic room where women might be screened. The examination would then comprise the probe being inserted into the vagina and run over the surface of the cervix: presumably, great care would have to be taken not to miss any areas. An advantage would be the instant result. However, a disadvantage would be the lack of any documented evidence of the examination: if it was not carried out properly, there would presumably be no way of knowing. I would imagine that such a careful examination of the cervix might necessitate the use of special couches, like those in colposcopy clinics.

Obviously, there is still a long way to go and many

details need to be sorted out. However, this is an exciting idea which deserves further investigation.

MORE ACCESSIBLE COLPOSCOPY?

At present, there is a great shortage of gynaecologists trained in colposcopy. Clinics are overflowing with patients, waiting lists in some areas are several months long. Women are anxious while waiting to be seen and the whole situation is unsatisfactory. What can be done?

Of course, one solution would be to train more gynaecologists. But it is very unlikely that they would want to do nothing other than colposcopy, and then there might be overstaffing in other fields as a result. All this could become very expensive.

Cervicography is an option, but has yet to become wholly accepted by the medical profession. Another alternative is to train doctors who are not gynaecologists but have had some gynaecological training. These could be GPs, family planning doctors and doctors working in genito-urinary medicine. Their advantage is that they are in any case likely to be dealing with women who have abnormal smears and are therefore both interested and experienced in this area.

It is important that such doctors are properly trained, and preferably spend at least some time in their local colposcopy unit. It is essential that a good working relationship exists between them and their gynaecological colleagues, since it is likely that treatments will have to be performed in the gynaecology department, and difficult cases will need to be managed jointly. Family planning clinics and departments of genito-urinary medicine are ideally placed for such collaborations; often doctors doing colposcopy in the clinic can arrange to do treatment sessions at the hospital, so that they can continue to look after their own patients. Women often find it less stressful to be seen in their usual clinic, where the surroundings are familiar and they know the reception staff, the nurses, and perhaps also the doctor who performs the colposcopy.

Colposcopy clinics have also realised the benefit of having doctors who come in for a few sessions a week just to do colposcopy. These may be GPs or family planning doctors, and they often remain in the job for years, providing continuity and reducing the need to keep training new junior doctors, who are going to move on in six months or a year. This is an increasing trend, and one which I hope will continue.

FINALLY

This is an exciting time in the field of cervical screening and colposcopy. There are a number of new ideas which seem to be promising and, what is more, may be in use within the next decade. However, in the interim, do not forget that the tried-and-tested, boring old cervical smear will still give you protection against cervical cancer – so make sure you go for yours.

Further reading

Positive Smear
Susan Quilliam
Charles Letts & Co. Ltd, 2nd edition 1992
Written by a woman who had an abnormal smear. She went on to interview other women and has collected their experiences into this book. There are many excerpts from the interviews, and helpful suggestions about how to cope emotionally right from the time you hear the result to after your treatment.

Prevention of Cervical Cancer: The patient's view
Tina Posner and Martin Vessey
King Edward's Hospital Fund for London, 1988
The results of a large survey of women's perceptions of and attitudes towards the whole issue of smears, colposcopy and treatment. Although written primarily for health professionals, it is quite easy to read and makes many pertinent observations.

The Best Counselling Guide
Susan Quilliam and Ian Grove-Stephenson
Thorsons, 1991
A consumer guide to counselling, with advice on how to obtain counselling and a comprehensive list of all the main counselling organisations in Great Britain.

*Hysterectomy: What it is, and how to cope with it
successfully*
Suzie Hayman
Sheldon Press
A very readable book that covers all aspects, both physical and emotional, of having a hysterectomy.

Contraception: A user's handbook
Dr Anne Szarewski and Professor John Guillebaud
Oxford University Press, 1994
A comprehensive guide to all methods of contraception, including discussions of health risks and benefits.

Useful addresses

UK

The Health Education Authority
Hamilton House
Mabledon Place
London WC1H 9TX
071 631 0930
Provides information and leaflets on all aspects of
women's health.

Scottish Health Education Group
Woodburn House
Canaan Lane
Edinburgh EH10 4SG
031 447 8044
Similar to the above.

The Family Planning Association
27–35 Mortimer Street
London W1N 7RJ
071 636 7866
Gives advice on all aspects of family planning and
sexual problems. A good source of information about
other clinics and services available throughout the
United Kingdom. They have a bookshop as well as free
leaflets on many topics.

Margaret Pyke Centre for Study and Training in Family
Planning
15 Bateman's Buildings
Soho Square
London W1V 5TW
071 734 9351
The largest centre in Europe, dealing with all aspects of
family planning, screening and counselling.

Brook Advisory Centres
Head Office
153a East Street
London SE17 2SD
071 708 1234
Specialise in young people's problems (under 24).
Provide family planning, screening services and coun-
selling.

British Association for Counselling
37a Sheep Street
Rugby
Warwickshire CV21 3BX
0788 578328
Useful source of nationwide information about clinics
that provide counselling.

Relate (formerly National Marriage Guidance Council)
Head Office
Herbert Gray College
Little Church Street
Rugby
Warwickshire CV21 3AP
0788 73241
Nationwide network of clinics providing psychosexual
and marriage guidance counselling. Local branches can

be found in telephone directories.

Scottish Marriage Guidance Council
26 Frederick Street
Edinburgh EH2 2JR
031 225 5006
Similar to Relate.

Association of Sexual and Marital Therapists
PO Box 62
Sheffield S10 3TS

Terence Higgins Trust
BM AIDS
London WC1N 3XX
071 833 2971 / 071 278 8745
Helpline 071 833 2971
Information, support groups and counselling about
AIDS.

The Herpes Association
41 North Road
London N7 9DP
071 609 9061

The Women's National Cancer Control Campaign
Suna House
128 Curtain Road
London EC2 3AR
071 729 4688
Information and free leaflets on all aspects of women's
cancers.

Women's Health Concern
Alexandra House
Oldham Terrace
London W3 6NH
071 938 3932
Practical help with women's health problems, es-
pecially those relating to the menstrual cycle and the
menopause.

Action on Smoking and Health (ASH)
109 Gloucester Place
London W1H 3PH
071 935 3519

Private Family Planning Clinics

Marie Stopes House
The Well Woman Centre
108 Whitfield Street
London W1P 6BE
071 388 0662/2585
Cervicography is available at all the Marie Stopes
Clinics.

Marie Stopes Centre
10 Queen Square
Leeds LS2 8AJ
0532 440685

Marie Stopes Centre
1 Police Street
Manchester
M2 7LQ
061 832 4250

Hanway Clinic
1 Hanway Place
London W1P 9DF
071 636 0366

EIRE

Irish Family Planning Clinic
Cathal Brugha Street Clinic
Dublin 1
Dublin 727276/727363
Provides a similar service to the FPA within the confines of Irish law.

UNITED STATES

Planned Parenthood Federation of America
Head Office
2010 Massachusetts Avenue
NW Suite 500
Washington DC 20036
202 785 3351

Western region:
333 Broadway, 3rd Floor
San Francisco
California 94133
415 956 8856

Southern region:
3030 Peachtree Road, NW Room 303
Atlanta
Georgia 30305

Northern region:
2625 Butterfield Road
Oak Brook
Illinois 60521
312 986 9270

AUSTRALIA

Australian Federation of FPAs
Suite 603, 6th floor
Roden Cutler House
24 Campbell Street
Sydney NSW 2000

NEW ZEALAND

The New Zealand FPA Inc.
PO Box 68200
214 Karangahape
Newton
Auckland

SOUTH AFRICA

FPA of South Africa
412 York House
46 Kerk Street
Johannesburg 2001

Index

Page numbers in *italic* refer to the illustrations

treatment, 79–80,
82–3
as warning sign, 100–1
bleomycin, 149
blood tests, 108, 109,
122–3, 133
bowels, 47, 53, 110–11
'breakthrough bleeding',
100–1
breast cancer, 125
British Medical Association
(BMA), 161–2

cancer: abnormal smears
and, 26, 28, 29–30
breast cancer, 125
causes, 114–29
cervical smears and, 10
chemotherapy, 112, 127
cone biopsy, 96
during pregnancy, 96–7
emotional reactions, 177,
186–8
incidence, 152–6, 153,
154, 163–5, 164
invasive, 107–8
microinvasion, 102–3,
104–7
Polarprobe, 211
radiotherapy, 110–12
spread of, 102–8, 105
stages, 102
success rates for
treatments, 112–13
surgery, 109–10
treatment, 99–113
viruses and, 133–50
warning signs, 100–1

candida, 20, 45–8, 56
Canesten, 48
carcinoma-in-situ, 25–6
catheters, urinary, 109–10
cautery, 83
cells: abnormal changes,
23–37, 24, 27
biopsy, 66–8, 67
cervical smear, 15–16
cervix, 7–10, 8, 9
effects of smoking, 121–2
endocervical, 38–43
HDA test, 205–6
inflammatory changes,
55–8
spread of cancer cells,
102–8, 105
viruses, 131, 136, 138–9
cervical ectopy, 43–5, 87,
100, 101, 175
cervical smears, 10–21
after laser and loop
diathermy treatment,
84
age at first smear, 163–5
age at last smear, 168–9
automated tests, 205–6
and cervicography,
203–4
emotional reactions,
174–9
examination of cells,
15–16
frequency, 156–63, 165,
167–8
getting the results,
169–72
instruments, 12, 12–14,

THE MENOPAUSE
A practical guide to understanding and coping with the change
Dr Jean Coope

The menopause is an inevitable event that faces a women as her fertile years decline. For some it is approached with confidence, for others it is a difficult time of transition and adjustment.

Dr Jean Coope, Family Planning advisor and Well-Women counsellor, has written this valuable and reassuring guide, answering many questions women raise on the menopause, including advice on HRT, exercise and keeping healthy, continuing an enjoyable sex life, and taking action against osteoporosis.

LIVING WITH ENDOMETRIOSIS
A practical guide to the causes and treatments
Caroline Hawkridge

Endometriosis is an increasingly common gynaecological disorder affecting an estimated one to two percent of all women of childbearing age. Left untreated it is a cause of pain, menstrual disorders and even infertility.

In this book, written in conjunction with the Endometriosis Society and a medical expert, Caroline Hawkridge provides the most up-to-date summary of the disease and all that is known about its cause, diagnosis and treatment. Sympathetic and comprehensive, the book covers: problems of diagnosis, how to manage pain, hormonal, surgical and alternative treatments, endometriosis and pregnancy, and understanding and managing your feelings.

PASSAGE TO POWER
Natural menopause revolution
Leslie Kenton

Now in the paperback edition, *Passage to Power* will continue to help the thousands of women who fear the menopause or who are suffering from menopausal trouble. A veritable bible of natural menopause, it tackles the science of menopause and scrutinizes the practices commonly associated with it. Leslie Kenton questions the benefits of HRT, examines the politics behind such treatments and sets out the principles of natural HRT.

The book describes the extraordinary healing powers of natural progesterone and reveals the devastating effects of xenoestrogens – environmental chemicals to which western women (and men) are increasingly exposed. Finally she shows women how to reconnect with their deepest levels of intuition and instinct on their journey towards individual freedom.

Passage To Power enables all women to face the menopause in possession of all the knowledge they need to live their lives to the full.

To order any of these books direct from Vermilion (p+p free), use the form below or call our credit-card hotline on **01279 427203**.

Please send me

...... copies of **BEAT CANDIDA** @ £8.99 each

...... copies of **TIRED ALL THE TIME** @ £8.99 each

...... copies of **THE MENOPAUSE** @ £8.99 each

...... copies of **LIVING WITH ENDOMETRIOSIS** @ £8.99 each

...... copies of **PASSAGE TO POWER** @ £9.99 each

Mr/Ms/Mrs/Miss/Other (Block Letters)

....

Address..

....

....

Postcode................................Signed................................

HOW TO PAY

☐ I enclose a cheque/postal order for

£............................... made payable to 'Vermilion'

☐ I wish to pay by Access/Visa card (delete where appropriate)

Card Number ☐☐☐☐☐☐☐☐☐☐☐☐☐☐☐☐

Expiry Date ☐☐☐☐

Post order to **Murlyn Services Ltd, PO Box 50, Harlow, Essex CM17 0DZ.**

POSTAGE AND PACKING ARE FREE. Offer open in Great Britain including Northern Ireland. Books should arrive less than 28 days after we receive your order; they are subject to availability at time of ordering. If not entirely satisfied return in the same packaging and condition as received with a covering letter within 7 days. Vermilion books are available from all good booksellers.